The World of Antiques

The World of Antiques

Hamlyn
London · New York · Sydney · Toronto

Plantagenet
Somerset Fry F.R.S.A.

Introduction by
Ralph and Terry Kovel

endpapers
Christie's Auction Room by Thomas Rowlandson (1756-1827),
from *The Microcosm of London*, Vol. I, published by Ackermann
of London in 1811.

1 *frontispiece*
Mr Peter Wilson, chairman of Sotheby's, London, auctions
The Temptation of Eve by Hans Baldung, at a picture sale on
December 3rd, 1969. The painting fetched £224,000 (about
$537,600). A little over seventy years ago it was valued at
£20 (about $48).

Published by
THE HAMLYN PUBLISHING GROUP LIMITED
London · New York · Sydney · Toronto
Hamlyn House, Feltham, Middlesex, England

© Copyright The Hamlyn Publishing Group Limited 1970

First Edition 1970
Third Impression 1971

ISBN 0 600 39202 3

Filmset by Filmtype Services Limited, Scarborough, Yorkshire
Printed in Italy by O.G.A.M., Verona

Contents

ntroduction

Antiques are many things to many people. We collectors are perhaps a little 'sick' in our own special way. Some of us want to amass hundreds of examples of Chelsea boxes, glass shoes, coffin markers, or just things. A true collector can only be differentiated from a miser hoarding his treasures by his intellectual approach to his collection. It is strange to want to own all the old boxes and cans used by an 1880 grocery store, but it is considered an intelligent, admirable occupation if the study of the boxes can reveal beauty, social mores, or historic trends. To be a collector who studies and regards antiques as a serious adjunct to life and to the arts, one must read and reread many books and sort and organize the information gleaned from them to fit the collection.

The average collector is neither historian nor art critic, but a perceptive person attuned to the aura of the past and interested in adding a new dimension to his present. For this collector, a large assortment of a single type of antique is of less use than a general collection which he can fit successfully into a practical home. Today, selective decorating enables one to use the furniture of many periods with accessories of humor, of distinction, and of differing ages. Many of the styles that can still be found in the antique world at reasonable prices are pictured and described in this book in terms not only of appearance, but also of use and cost. Can you sit comfortably in a chair of a certain style? Would it be good as a dining room table chair or to fill a seldom-used corner of the living room?

Every study of pottery and porcelain must lead us back to the European and especially the English factories of the 18th and 19th centuries. It is only within this historical frame of reference that a collector can gain the confidence to buy the later English and American wares. To be a critic of any art form and to know what is good and what is not, you must understand the beginning of the art form and the signs of quality. A single blue-and-white bowl by Spode or a Derby tea set can often be found in shops at prices lower than the companies' present-day reproduction of the old designs. The knowledgeable collector can sense the difference between the old and the new, and he can appreciate the subtle superiority of the original pieces.

Some collectors claim that a room is not 'alive' without the tick of an antique clock. Many decorators and collectors, including us, declare with vigor that if you cannot afford a really fine painting, it is far better to avoid a reproduction of it and buy a fine original old print. The gleam of silver, copper, brass, or glass can add a sparkle to any room. Learning which of these pieces to buy is difficult, but with study and with these hints on how to start looking, a beginner can avoid some costly mistakes.

It is the 'miscellaneous' antiques that really express the taste and personality of a collector. Some say that really to know a person, one must examine the titles of the books in his library. We prefer a quick look at the 'etcetera' scattered throughout the house. A house filled with chessmen must be more intellectual than the house decorated with swords. A collector of needlework will certainly be more appreciative of handicrafts, but in a way quite different, than the owner of several small inlaid wooden tea caddies.

Antiques should be loved, admired, and used. They must be understood and studied until you can determine which pieces in the wide world of antiques can best express your thoughts and appeal to your aesthetic sense.

Shaker Heights,
Ohio,
1970

Ralph and Terry Kovel
(authors of *Complete
Antiques Price Lists*)

The Collector's World

The saleroom was crowded. Dealers, collectors, experts and newspapermen jostled with each other and with saleroom staff as they examined the array of paintings and drawings that were about to be auctioned. Somewhere towards the back of the room sat a Scottish teacher who had entered a painting for sale because she wanted to buy a new car. It was *The Temptation of Eve* 1 by Hans Baldung, a little-known 16th-century German artist, and it had been valued at the end of the last century for only £20. Her uncle had left it to her.

Suddenly the auctioneer rapped the gavel on his rostrum and called for the sale to begin. Various lots went swiftly to this and that purchaser or to his agent, and then the auctioneer reached the German painting. The bidding began briskly. Up and up it went: £60,000, £80,000, £100,000. The teacher had been told by the experts before the sale to expect the painting to fetch about £100,000, but amid mounting tension the bidding continued and soon broke through £200,000. The auctioneer finally reached £224,000, and called out the vast sum once, twice, three times, in a clear, firm voice. Then down came the gavel, and the painting was sold to Messrs Agnew, the art dealers.

What does this amazing good luck for the Scottish teacher show? It shows that a work of art, consigned to the attic, or sold off for a small sum a generation or two ago through ignorance or indifference, can still fetch a fortune today. It also reflects changing tastes in the world of art and antiques. Eighty years ago the German painter Hans Baldung was hardly known, and his work was regarded as of little value. Today, almost any painter of the 16th century is important.

Exactly the same can, and does, happen with antiques, whether furniture, china, glass, clocks, metalwork, prints, or miscellanea. It may not be easy to buy a piece for a song in a junk shop, or find one among grandmother's things after she has died, and promptly sell it for hundreds or thousands of pounds or dollars. But bargains are still obtainable, and you may be perhaps the more likely to find one if you are armed with a little more knowledge of the world of antiques than other people. This book has been written to provide you with some of that knowledge.

Purchasing antiques is an investment; indeed, it becomes an increasingly reliable and profitable investment every year. Rich connoisseurs pay for one piece sums of money equivalent to the total earnings of an ordinary man throughout his working life. They do so

2
The Portobello Road antique market, London, on a Saturday afternoon. This is one of the most famous areas in the world for collecting.

3
Typical country antique shop in the United States. This one is at Gatlinburg, Tennessee.

Numbers in the margins refer to illustrations mentioned in the text

2

3

6

4 *(page 14)*
Perhaps the most famous piece of furniture in the world, the Bureau du Roi, made for Louis XV by J. F. Oeben and J. H. Riesener between 1760 and 1769. Versailles.

5 *(page 15)*
One of a pair of bonheurs-du-jour, made by Martin Carlin in about 1770, which obtained a record price for a furniture item at a sale, namely 82,000 guineas (about $206,640) at Christie's, London, in June 1967.

6
American silver tankard and cover made by Josiah Austin of Charlestown, Massachusetts. The scroll handle is engraved with the initials 'HBE' and dated 1740. In November 1965, the tankard was sold at auction for £1,050 (about $2,520).

7
Pair of Meissen figures which fetched £25,365 (about $60,876) in Geneva on October 2nd, 1969.

not only because the object is a work of art; they also look to selling it in future years at a substantial profit and buying something even better. At the end of the 1939–45 war the distinguished author Cecil Woodham Smith invested in a large quantity of Georgian furniture which came up for sale here and there at cheap prices. In the 1950s her collection was sold at a very considerable profit.

Early in the 19th century French furniture made by the Paris craftsmen of the 18th century was sometimes sold for less than it had cost to make. But throughout the 19th century and since, the value has increased, and now it costs a great deal more than any other kind. A pair of bonheurs-du-jour by Martin Carlin, decorated **5** with Sèvres porcelain plaques which were signed by the makers, fetched the record price for a furniture item of 82,000 guineas (about $206,640) at a sale of French furniture at Christie's, London, in June 1967. This was the famous sale where the world's richest man, Paul Getty, who was attending, sat in a Louis XV chair.

The chair was sold for a few hundred pounds, and someone from the floor asked the auctioneer, 'Does that include the contents?'

You are very unlikely to come across real 18th-century French furniture in sales other than at Sotheby's or Christie's in London or at Parke-Bernet's in New York, except on the rarest occasions, and you will not find pieces in more than a handful of dealers' showrooms. It has been estimated that a total of about 100,000 pieces were made by all the Paris craftsmen working between the years 1680 and 1800. This is not many, and most of those that have not been destroyed are now in museums or in private collections.

11 French furniture is regarded now as the finest ever made. You have only to see the Jones Collection in the Victoria and Albert Museum, or the Wallace Collection, London, to understand why. It may not be to everybody's taste, but there is no questioning the supremacy of the skill and craftsmanship of the Paris furniture-makers. Perhaps the most famous piece of

furniture ever made is the Bureau du Roi, a roll-top **4** writing desk specially constructed for Louis XV. It was started in about 1760 by Jean François Oeben, the leading cabinet-maker of his time. He died in 1763, and his widow authorised his senior assistant, Jean Henri Riesener, to finish it. Other experts also helped with the mounts. In 1768 Oeben's widow married Riesener, who completed the desk the next year. He was to become the leading cabinet-maker of his time, and is considered by some as the finest of them all. In my view it is impossible to put a price on this piece. It must be worth at least £1,000,000 or $2,400,000.

An enormous number of copies of 18th-century French styles were made in the 19th century in England, France, Germany and elsewhere, and for the untrained eye it is impossible to see the difference. Since there are literally only half-a-dozen people in the world who really know 18th-century French furniture – and not one of them is associated in any way with dealer or auction room – many of the copies appear in the sales

masquerading, quite innocently, as genuine articles. There is an astonishing ignorance of French furniture in the antique trade. Should you ever become wealthy enough to start collecting—and even the smaller and simpler pieces will cost very high sums—it is essential to get help from the Wallace Collection, the Victoria and Albert Museum, or A. T. Dell, perhaps the only independent American authority on the subject. This does not alter the fact that the 19th-century copies are often very good indeed and worth collecting for their own sake. In twenty or thirty years, they will constitute antiques themselves.

In the English furniture field the three major styles of the 18th century are named after Thomas Chippendale, George Hepplewhite and Thomas Sheraton. Of these, only Chippendale actually made any furniture that we know of, and these articles are rare. They are almost all either in museums or in a few large private houses, such as Harewood House or Woburn Abbey. On the rare occasions when they do appear in salerooms they reach very high figures.

We know little about Hepplewhite's life, and his fame is really posthumous. Two years after his death in 1786, his widow published a book of his drawings of furniture called *The Cabinet-Maker and Upholsterer's Guide*. This immortalised his name, and a vast amount of furniture based on his designs was made and is called Hepplewhite. Similarly with Sheraton; no piece can actually be attributed to him. His book *The Cabinet-Maker's and Upholsterer's Drawing-Book*, published in parts between 1791 and 1794, enjoyed great popularity and established his name. Thereafter, much English furniture followed his ideas, and the years from about 1795 to about 1810 are known as the Sheraton period. Despite this, you will find many a piece that may resemble his patterns marked 'Sheraton, *c.* 1785'. Beware of this inaccuracy. It has been used before now to justify a higher price for a copy that ought to be marked 'Sheraton, *c.* 1795'.

It may seem a trivial point, but inaccuracies like this merely indicate the possibilities of inaccuracies elsewhere. Some dealers are unfortunately not very knowledgeable about the things they sell. The essence of their activity is buying something and selling it to someone else for more than they paid. Profit is the principal, sometimes the sole, objective. They become adept at knowing what the public wants, but, in fact, if you look into it a little closely you find that what the public wants is what dealers have to sell; that is, dealers tend to create rather than fulfil demand.

If you are going to collect any of the things described in this or any other book, of course you will have to go from time to time to dealers. The best advice is to be sure you are armed with a little knowledge, which you can get from a wide range of books, many of which are in the list at the end of this book. If you decide, for example, to collect English copperware, do brief yourself before you go to a dealer. Time and again you will find an ale jug or a kettle marked 'antique 18th century', but, as you will see in the chapter on copper and brass, there is very little 18th-century copper left in England and it is almost entirely in museums. It was very well copied in the 19th century and even beaten to make it look a hundred years older.

Somehow the phrase '18th century' has a sort of magic about it. Put it on a piece of indeterminate household ware and it immediately enwraps the piece with authenticity. It is of course very difficult to distinguish between later 18th century and early 19th century in many antiques. Some early 19th-century porcelain and pottery is just as fine and attractive as late 18th-century examples, particularly Swansea and Nantgarw.

Do not forget that you can always try to bargain with a dealer. He may or may not like it, but he will expect it. The secret is to make an offer of, for instance, between 10 and 20 per cent lower than the price on the tag and accept 10 per cent. You will be able to do this more confidently if you have read up the background of the particular antiques for which you are searching. If you were 'in the trade', you would be allowed up to 40 per cent discount, which shows how much profit a dealer can make on his stock. In fact, a recent survey showed that the average dealer in Britain had to operate on a 70 to 80 per cent profit basis in order to stay in business, although the junk dealer can manage on less than 50 per cent. One does not want to pillory the dealers, but it is the public, looking for an investment or simply a few beautiful and antique articles, who pays the money, and should therefore be protected. Unfortunately there are no guarantees that you get what you pay for.

An examination of the prices fetched at salerooms over a period of, say, twelve months, is perhaps the surest way to establish values, or at least prices. On the whole you will do better at salerooms than at dealers. To begin with, dealers obtain much of their stock from salerooms. Secondly, although the evils of the auction 'ring' still persist here and there, the average sale is safe. Certainly the more reputable salerooms do not tolerate 'ring' activities. Articles can be examined closely a day or two before the sale actually takes place, and you will not normally be interrupted if you pick up a piece of porcelain and hold it up to the light to gauge its translucency. You may also bring in an expert-friend for his opinion, and no embarrassment will be caused. As a rule the auction room staff will be very helpful. Many of them have gained from long experience a shrewd understanding of antiques, and they can judge, in an uncanny but often accurate way, whether or not a

8
Candelabra-vase probably designed by Claude Duplessis for Madame de Pompadour and made at Sèvres in 1756. Wallace Collection, London.

9

9
Pair of 18th-century painted ivory fans sold for £150 ($360) at Sotheby's, London, in February 1968. The one above has a scene of King Charles III of Sicily and his wife, Maria Amalia, riding in a carriage. The one below shows an interior view of a saleroom after Rowlandson.

10

10
Clock by Vulliamy enclosed in a glass case, on a satinwood stand. The panel in the stand was painted by Cipriani in about 1780.

11
Louis XV bedroom at the Château de Champs, near Paris.

piece is what it is claimed to be. What is more, if you ask them, for example, how much an early 19th-century longcase clock made by Roberts of Bangor is likely to fetch, they will often give you a price that is surprisingly near to what it actually achieves in the saleroom later.

Attending a sale is an exhilarating business, especially if there are one or two articles that you want to buy. But you need to be careful not to be carried away by the enthusiasm of the moment. You should decide before the sale begins what is the maximum price that you want to pay, based either on the help of your expert-friend or on an average calculated on prices obtained for similar articles at other sales. If the bidding reaches your maximum very quickly indeed, then you should probably forget about the article, for it may be sold for as much as twice your figure. If, on the other hand, the bidding slows down below your figure, then watch carefully. If it creeps above your price, raise your bid, but do not do so with any sign of enthusiasm. Try to appear indifferent. Many people at auction sales bid almost entirely on the reactions of others. They may also be carried away with 'auction room fever'. Let the bidding go to about 25 per cent higher before giving up. You should be safe if you get the piece at that price, for if a dealer were to get the article at your price he would add his percentage before selling it again in his shop. I have been collecting odds and ends at auction sales at various places for ten years or more, and I cannot say that there is one occasion when I feel that I have really spent too much. I have also been perfectly happy with prices which I have obtained in sales for pieces I have put in, even allowing for the auctioneers' commissions, which vary between 10 and 15 per cent.

When selling more valuable pieces, which would normally be offered through Sotheby's or Christie's or one or two other major auctioneers, you may have to wait some time before it comes up for sale. You will be advised to pick the most suitable sale, which could be several weeks ahead. If the piece is sold to your satisfaction, another few weeks will elapse before you receive payment. Do not blame the auctioneer if your piece does not reach the reserve price you put on it. It does not necessarily mean that the piece is not worth it; possibly there were not enough dealers or collectors who wished to buy it, and it may well reach your asking price, or more, in a subsequent sale.

It will be seen in the text that, apart from some American articles that are of special interest, descriptions generally stop at about 1840. From the British Board of Trade's point of view an article is considered an antique if it is certificated as being a hundred or more years old. But 1830 has for some years been the latest date acceptable to organisers of antique fairs, and this date has generally been followed by antique dealers. Victoriana, therefore, is excluded, and it is well written up in a number of other works, some of which are in the list at the end of this book. This does not detract from the undoubted qualities of many Victorian things, especially a good deal of mid 19th-century porcelain and pottery.

Antique fairs are not the best places to find bargains, nor are they really the source for articles at reasonable prices. Anyone who has a stand at an antiques fair adds 10 or 20 per cent to the price of most of his goods. There is the cost of the stand, which is high, there is the transportation of articles for display to and from the shop, and sometimes there is elegant literature to print. And, of course, since the average person expects to have to spend more at a fair, up goes the price.

In 1960 I bought at an auction room a very badly damaged Hepplewhite-style card table. It was described as 'an 18th-century Hepplewhite card table . . . (A.F.)'. A.F. means 'As Found', a euphemistic way of saying 'damaged'. I paid fifty shillings (about $6), after taking along with me to the saleroom a day before a well-known furniture restorer who said that the table was really too damaged to be worth repairing. Nevertheless, I liked the piece. For four years I kept it in a garage. Then I found a retired ship's carpenter who repaired antique furniture, more for the love of the work than for the money. He had the table for nearly a year, and at the end had rendered it almost in an original condition, for £17 10s. (about $40). I kept the table for another year and then tried to sell it to a number of dealers. The best price I was offered was £45 (about $108). In 1966 I persuaded a standholder at an antiques fair to put it on the stand on a sale or return basis, at $12\frac{1}{2}$ per cent commission. The table was sold on the first day for £80 (about $192), which I should say was about £10 ($24) more than one could have safely asked in most shops.

On the whole the high point of British design and craftsmanship in household things extends roughly from the decade 1750–60 to the decade 1810–20. In the earlier decade a significant upsurge occurred in furniture, porcelain, pottery and glass, while clocks and silver from Britain had for some time been the best obtainable in Europe. These are seen to decline after about 1815, when, despite the great victory at Waterloo, Britain – together with the whole of Europe – was plunged into a prolonged period of trade recession. This coincided with the growth of mechanisation, and machine-made things were made much more quickly than hand-made things.

This period of 60 or 70 years was prolific as well as creative. All over Britain leading styles were imitated

The Etruscan Room at Osterley Park, Middlesex, designed by Robert Adam in about 1775. The design is typical of Adam's Neo-Classical innovations in England in the second half of the 18th century.

13
The McIntire Room at the H. F. du Pont Winterthur Museum, Delaware.

14
Chippendale mirror of about 1760–70 in the Chinese style.

and adapted, not only in furniture but also in china, glass, clocks and silver, and a considerable amount of the production of the period has survived. Naturally prices increase every year, but there seems to be, whatever dealers may tell you, an almost inexhaustible supply. The number of sales held each year by auctioneers has not decreased, nor has the number of items in the catalogues for each sale.

It is therefore as good a time to collect as it ever has been. The habit is catching. There are many more antique shops than there were five years ago and special magazines are published regularly for trade and public. Interest in top sales at Sotheby's and Christie's grows; high prices are frequently reported on radio and television news programmes. Even women's magazines are now including regular features on things to collect.

This publicity is good. It is breeding a new type of person, the amateur 'expert', who keenly seeks out the information available in an ever-expanding number of books of reference. And this will help keep the dealers better informed, which, in turn, will go some way towards improving the image of the antique trade. 'The customer is always right' is the guiding principle of trade; if, in the world of antiques, he cannot always be right, he should never be *wronged*.

Furniture

Furniture is by far the most popular category of antiques. For every dealer who specialises in china there are ten who deal in furniture, and for every book on silver or glass there are five or more on furniture styles. And yet it cannot really be collected in the same way as the other articles dealt with in this book. No-one would really think of accumulating break-front bookcases or Knole sofas, and only a wealthy few can afford to collect real 18th-century French commodes.

Perhaps the most satisfactory way, therefore, to indulge your taste for beautiful furniture, which need not always be expensive, is to set out to furnish your home with it. Apart from a soft bed, you can find every piece you need amongst 18th- and early 19th-century furniture. Inexpensive pieces are still quite easily obtainable at dealers and at salerooms, but of course considerable caution should be exercised before signing your cheque for a well-polished sofa table marked 'circa 1810' which was probably made in 1960, or a set of four Sheraton dining chairs – you will remember he never made any furniture at all.

Furniture is almost always functional, though it is not always elegant. It has been made by every country in nearly every age in civilised history. There is a chair in the Cairo Museum on which the Pharaoh Tutankhamen sat about 3,500 years ago. More than forty individual styles have emerged from Europe and the Near East alone, from the fall of the Roman Empire to 1830. But in this chapter we shall be looking only at the sort of furniture you can buy – or see, or read about someone else buying – in Britain or America, that is, chiefly English, Welsh, American, and some French. An 18th-century Polish cupboard is not likely to find its way into the English market, and I doubt if the Chinese would let you bring back from Peking a mandarin's chair of the Ming dynasty.

Starting with the main room of the house, the drawing room, let us see what sort of pieces would be needed and what can be found. Since people sit down in drawing rooms, you need a sofa, armchairs, and perhaps a few upright chairs. There are not many antique sofa styles. Thomas Chippendale, George Hepplewhite and Thomas Sheraton all designed what were called settees. Chippendale's were often large, heavy-looking, luxuriously upholstered, with cabriole legs (usually four in front and four at the back), serpentine-top back, and scroll arms. You will not get an original anywhere since he probably never made any himself, but some were produced in his workshop by one of his sons or by another employee in St Martin's Lane in London. But the occasional copy comes up sometimes in salerooms.

Hepplewhite's settees were much more delicate in

15
Welsh *cwpwrdd tridarn* from Flintshire. End of the 17th century. Private Collection.

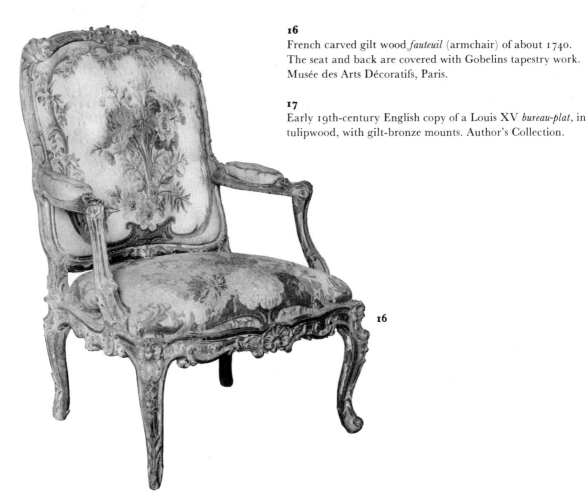

16

French carved gilt wood *fauteuil* (armchair) of about 1740.
The seat and back are covered with Gobelins tapestry work.
Musée des Arts Décoratifs, Paris.

17

Early 19th-century English copy of a Louis XV *bureau-plat*, in
tulipwood, with gilt-bronze mounts. Author's Collection.

16

appearance. The backs were sometimes shaped like the
Chippendale ones, but gracefully curved down at the
ends and running straight into the legs, which were
usually turned and tapering, sometimes fluted and
reeded. Hepplewhite never made any, but several
cabinet-makers of the late 18th and early 19th century
fashioned them according to his designs. An early 19th-
century copy fetched £85 (about $204) in a sale in 1967.

Sheraton designed upholstered settees which had
bolsters at each end, a style that continued to be popular
right up to 1830. Sometimes the framework was mahogany, sometimes giltwood, with the seat rail and
arm supports carved. The legs again were tapering,
square or rounded.

Upholstered antique armchairs are not very common, and perhaps the best-known are the wing chairs.
These are high-backed, with stuffed arms and wings.
They first appeared in the time of Charles II and have
been in demand ever since. The style has altered little.
The earliest ones, almost unobtainable in their original
state, had short cabriole legs. A Chippendale-style
mahogany wing chair of the 18th century recently
fetched £420 (about $1,008). A good 19th-century
copy, however, would be much cheaper.

16 French armchairs (*fauteuils*) of the Louis XV period
of furniture (*c.* 1735–*c.* 1760) are perhaps the most
elegant chairs ever made. They were generally of walnut, which was sometimes gilded or painted. Originals,

stamped or unstamped, are extremely rare, and even in
singles can fetch high prices at sales. But a number of
good copies were produced in the 19th century, not
only in France but also in England, and these would be
much cheaper.

Chippendale designed a variety of armchairs in the
French style, and these had upholstered backs, part-
covered arms, and large seats widening from back to
front, on cabriole legs. The mahogany woodwork was
elaborately carved, often in Chippendale's own idea of
the Rococo style. A good 18th-century chair made from
one of these designs can be found, but examples do not
come up for sale every day. Upright chairs, designs for
which Chippendale, Hepplewhite and Sheraton are all
famous, belong more to the dining room, discussed
later in this chapter.

Another important article for the drawing room is
the desk. If the room is large enough you may be able to
have two, one for the husband and one for the wife.
Eighteenth-century cabinet-makers paid much attention to this point, and in France – and to a lesser extent
in England – they devised a number of desk types that **5**
were meant for women to use.

The most widely used desk is the bureau with sloping
fall-front. These desks were first made in England in the
17th century. The Spanish had long before made their
vargueño, a writing cabinet with drawers, cupboards and
recesses, with a straight fall-front, the whole box being

17

placed on a separate table. The idea then was that the box could be moved from room to room – or house to house – and put down on whatever table could be spared to get on with one's writing. Then it occurred to someone to design something which combined box and table, and so was born the bureau. Developments followed, and early in the 18th century in England the bureau had three or four drawers – like a chest of drawers – surmounted by a section devoted to pigeon-holes and small drawers, enclosed by a sloping front. Bureaux in England were first made in walnut and the Welsh made some very fine ones in oak. As time went on refinements appeared. The pigeon-hole arrangement included secret compartments for papers and treasures – there were no safes then. The table part in front of the pigeon-hole section had a sliding platform which, when slid open, revealed a well that provided more means for concealment.

The bureau itself then acquired a superstructure, making the whole piece 6, 7, or even 8 feet tall. This superstructure was a cupboard arrangement for books, china or glass, though usually for books, and it had a variety of door-fronts: plain glass enclosed in wooden frames, lattice-paned, silvered glass, or just plain wood, or figured panels. The tops were provided with ornate or plain pediments and cornices. These articles were called bureau-bookcases, and they were made in walnut or mahogany. Quite a few of the original ones

appear in shops or salerooms, but are expensive. Fine, well-proportioned copies of later date can be obtained more cheaply.

There are two things to bear in mind when considering bureau-bookcases. First, only a largish drawing room, say, more than 18 feet by 15 feet with a ceiling 9 feet high or more, will really take the usual size, measuring 3 feet 6 inches to 4 feet wide and 6 feet 6 inches to 7 feet 6 inches high, with any comfort. If your main room is smaller, look for the smaller article, about 2 feet 10 inches to 3 feet 2 inches wide, and just under 6 feet high. These smaller ones are rather fine in proportion.

Occasionally the larger ones do not have a fall-front, but the top drawer of the chest part is a pigeon-hole and small drawer arrangement, with the front of the drawer falling to horizontal at the press of two recessed buttons. This type is usually called a secretaire bookcase.

Secondly, if you are really going to use the bureau, or secretaire, for regular writing, or even typing with a portable typewriter placed on a thick mat, but at the same time keep china or glass in the top part, then you need a robust piece, which probably means the larger variety. These are, on the whole, the easier ones to buy. With the conversion of so many large houses into smaller apartments, there is an increasing demand for smaller articles of furniture.

Another 18th-century desk type is the kneehole desk.

This was a table with drawers under the top and descending to the ground on either side, with a central space in which the sitter could put his knees. Sometimes this central space had a cupboard at the rear.

French gentlemen were provided with the *bureau-plat*, a flat table with two or three drawers under the top and with long cabriole legs from about 1720 to about 1765, and with straight, tapering legs after that. The rim of the table was encircled with gilt bronze and the corners similarly decorated. The top was almost always fitted with leather sheeting over the whole area except for a 2 to 3 inch border of wood. An original *bureau-plat* is extremely hard to get, and would cost a good deal of money. A stamped one fetched £20,833 (about $50,000) at a sale in London in December 1967. But several English firms of the early 19th century imitated these *bureaux-plats* very well. They were made usually of kingwood or tulipwood veneer. The larger ones are 6 to 7 feet wide, and the smaller ones about 4 feet 6 inches to 5 feet.

18
A semicircular card table of the 18th century. Royal Pavilion, Brighton.

19
Rosewood sofa table, made in about 1810. Royal Pavilion, Brighton.

20
Sheraton-style Pembroke table of maplewood, made in the last decade of the 18th century. Private Collection.

Another desk of interest is the Carlton House table. This was invented towards the end of the 18th century for one of the Prince of Wales's homes. Contrary to general belief, it was not originated by Sheraton, although he did include several designs for such desks in his book. They are usually made of mahogany inlaid with satinwood, or of satinwood, and they are handsome pieces. Good early 19th-century copies can be found.

The drawing room is not complete without a table or two. Tables were made in a variety of shapes and sizes for a multitude of purposes, in mahogany or in walnut, plain or with marquetry, or inlaid or banded, sometimes in satinwood. Flowers always enhance a room, and do so much more if placed in a vase upon an elegant table. One of the best kind of tables for this is the half-moon or semicircular side table, or its relative the half-moon card table, which has a flap with the same dimensions as the top so that it can be opened out to make a circle. These tables are in mahogany, plain or inlaid, and usually have square, tapering legs which may have satinwood inlay on the fronts near the top. The apron under the top may also be inlaid, either with simple lines of wood, or with festoons of flowers, or the same patterns may be painted on the surface. The card tables have green baize or black leather on the underside of the top flap and on the upper part of the lower flap as well.

18   19

The side tables generally came in pairs. Card tables, also made in pairs, can be obtained singly nowadays, and in 1968, at a good country saleroom in Britain, a fine tulipwood-banded mahogany example on square legs and measuring 3 feet 2 inches wide, fetched only £44 (about $105). The plainer ones can be bought for less in Britain.

Sometimes you will notice that the tops of these tables have become warped through lack of care over the years or perhaps because they have been in centrally-heated houses for some time. Not much can be done about this, unless you take it to a good cabinet-maker who will have to charge quite a high sum for a major repair job. If you are very keen to have a particular one which happens to be warped, take a cabinet-maker along with you to the shop before you buy.

There are, of course, several other kinds of small tables which equally well take flowers in a vase, or newspapers, or a choice piece of fine porcelain. One of the most popular is the sofa table. This is a rectangular table occasionally having two drawers under the centre part, with hinged flaps at each end. The whole is supported either by a central pedestal which at the lower end branches out into an arrangement of four feet, or a bracket arrangement at each end of the centre piece, joined by a stretcher. Such a bracket might be a lyre, or a plain upright on splayed feet.

Sofa tables first appeared towards the end of the 18th century. Both Hepplewhite and Sheraton designed

them. Today an 18th-century piece will be expensive, but a good 19th-century copy might be found for much less. Beware of a number of imitations made in the East End of London out of mahogany or rosewood planks left out on the roof for several months to accumulate 'wear' and 'patina'. Regency sofa tables (*c.* 1800–*c.* 1830) were often made of rosewood, and had brass inlay patterns round the top edges and down the legs or pedestals. **19**

Another elegant table for any drawing room is the Pembroke table, named not after the county, but a **20** Lady Pembroke. This is a small table on four square, tapering legs (later sometimes on four turned, plain or reeded legs), with fairly short flaps which were semi-circular, square with rounded ends, serpentine-ended, or square-ended. They are usually in mahogany with satinwood, boxwood, or even ebony inlay, or in satin-wood with marquetry of different woods. Sometimes they were made of pinewood lacquered in black and gold. There is usually one drawer at one end, and a dummy drawer end at the other.

A satinwood Pembroke table, after a design by Sheraton, fetched £175 (about $420) in a 1968 London saleroom, but in Britain you can get a plainer mahogany one, probably made in the early 19th century, for very much less. The oval ones are more difficult to find.

Since the main room has at least four corners, you need really to put something that fits snugly into one or two of them. Corner-cupboards were devised especi-

20

ally to absorb this otherwise wasted space. At first they were made in oak and walnut in late 17th-century days. Then in the middle of the 18th century they were made in mahogany. They were flat-fronted or bow-fronted – the latter are perhaps more attractive and certainly more expensive – and they had three or four shelves, enclosed by one or two doors. The shelves had flat, rounded, or serpentine front edges. Sometimes corner-cupboards were two-tiered. The top had a lattice-paned door or pair of doors covering shelves, under a moulded cornice. The bottom half had a solid panel door or doors with or without inlay or marquetry.

The more delicate lattice-paned, two-tier cupboards in mahogany are expensive. But they also come in oak or pine. Oak and pine single cupboards are also fairly easy to find, and in 1969 a bow-fronted oak one, with its original brass hinges, was sold in Britain for only £14 (about $33). In 19th-century England some 18th-century oak corner-cupboards, and 19th-century ones, too, were lacquered on the outside. The insides were also painted bright green or orange. A dealer in Essex removed the lacquer on several of these pieces and found underneath good oak panelling with a central shell motif inlay and oval and shell inlay design in the corners. I paid £8 (about $19) for one of these cupboards in 1961 to a Berkshire dealer, but I have not yet had the courage to remove the lacquer, because I rather like it as it is.

21 French corner-cupboards, called *encoignures*, generally came in pairs, with marble tops, and the doors were single or double. Again they might be flat or bow-fronted, and the decoration was invariably very rich and beautiful, at least up to the end of the Louis XVI period. Doors might be Chinese lacquered (straight from China), or veneered in kingwood or tulipwood with exquisite marquetry. A fine pair by J. F. Oeben, one of the best of the Paris cabinet-makers, is in the Victoria and Albert Museum, London. If a similar piece ever came on the market, it would fetch a very high figure.

There are a number of other pieces that you can put in the drawing room, such as a brass-bound, oval or octagonal, mahogany wine cooler on splayed feet, or a mahogany wine table with pie-crust rim and fluted pillar supported by cabriole legs, or a mahogany or rosewood Canterbury. A Canterbury is a late 18th-century innovation, a stand with partitions for music books, mounted on castors, occasionally with drawers. Such pieces are widely used nowadays for periodicals, and perhaps they are a little too highly priced for what they are.

There is one piece of furniture that many even modest collectors or antique-lovers long to own, and that is a French 18th-century commode, or a 19th-century copy of one. It is indeed a magnificent piece of 32 furniture. *Commode* is the French word for chest of drawers, and it is the most widely known article of 18th-century French furniture, if it is not always the most beautiful or elegant. Genuine 18th-century commodes do not often appear in salerooms, but if they do, they fetch very high prices if stamped and if the stamp can be shown to be genuine. One by Martin Carlin fetched £17,000 (about $40,800) at Sotheby's, London, in December 1967. A number of simpler and less ornate pieces were made in the provinces, and these do from time to time appear even in English shops.

Some of the articles mentioned so far were also made in oak, like the corner-cupboards, or fall-front bureaux. This usually suggests that they were made in the country, and generally they are not so well finished. Oak is a very difficult wood to use. If you have an old country cottage, with exposed rafters and studs in the drawing room, it is not necessary to fill the rooms with oak or fruitwood furniture, which is often less well made and less perfectly finished than the mahogany, walnut or rosewood. You can, in fact, mix the country pieces with the town pieces. It is not so much the different woods that could clash as the periods of furniture. Almost any good piece of the period 1650 to 1830 goes well with another of the same two centuries. The clash comes when antique furniture is mixed with Victorian or 20th-century furniture, though there are a few exceptions. Victorian balloon-back, upright chairs with cabriole legs have an air of Frenchness and look well with a rosewood, round dining table of Regency date.

Another important room in the house is the dining room, and this brings us to two more articles, upright chairs and dining tables. You will almost certainly have more chairs than any other article of furniture in the house, for they can be put in every room except, perhaps, the kitchen and bathroom, but even here you can get delicate, white-painted Victorian chairs with turned splayed legs which look right. Chairs are perhaps the only article of furniture that you can begin to collect in the same way as glasses, except that space will limit the number you can accumulate.

Chippendale, Hepplewhite, Adam, and Sheraton all designed a considerable range of upright chairs. They were made in sets for dining rooms, in eight, twelve or fourteen. The sets included one or more carver chairs, that is, uprights with arms. The best sets were invariably made to order for the owners of famous homes such as Harewood House, Stoneleigh Abbey, Woburn Abbey and Longleat. Sets like these are usually substantiated by the bills sent by the makers, which provide one of the very few ways to establish authenticity. Many sets were divided up for one reason or another, and from time to time twos, fours and sixes appear on the market. They are still very expensive, but to buy a pair that could be proved genuine would be a good investment.

Chairs have been the subject of whole books, and only

21
Mid 18th-century French *encoignure* (corner-cupboard) with bow-front panel of Chinese lacquer, gilt-bronze mounts and marble surmount. Wallace Collection, London.

the briefest summary can be included here. Leaving aside the walnut chairs of the late 17th and early 18th centuries, which in original form are rare, there was a great vogue for chair design and manufacture from about the middle of the 18th century. This was exemplified chiefly by the designs of Chippendale, Hepplewhite and Sheraton. Roughly, Chippendale's chairs, recommended to be made in mahogany, were square in appearance. The backs were wider at the top than at the bottom, that is, wedge-shaped, the top rails being bow-shaped. This framework enclosed a great variety of designs in the Chinese, Rococo and Gothic style, incorporating splatwork, fretwork, ribband patterns (knots with bows) and ladder-back designs. The legs were either heavy cabriole, with carving on the knees, sometimes ending in ball and claw feet, or square and straight, with chamfered edges on the inside. Seats were often over-stuffed and covered in leather which was ornamented with brass studding round the edges. Chippendale's own designs in most cases had carving on the backs. Good 18th-century copies of his work are expensive. A set of six chairs fetched £400 (about $960)

at a sale in 1967, and this figure would now be about half as much again.

Hepplewhite's chair designs are more delicate looking. He was greatly influenced by the Classical Revival initiated by Robert Adam in the 1760s and 1770s (as was Chippendale, also, in his last years). Hepplewhite's chairs are distinctly different from Chippendale's. The whole chair is lighter, and the legs, sometimes turned, sometimes square, are gracefully tapering and very narrow. The carving is not as elaborate as Chippendale's, and motifs are generally Classical, with urns, swags and medallions. The backs are oval or shield-shaped – the shield back is especially associated with Hepplewhite – with a variety of splats, such as Prince of Wales ostrich feathers, moulded upright struts, or wheel spokes radiating from the centre. The top rail often rises in the centre.

Sheraton's designs are straighter than Hepplewhite's, and the chairs seem lighter still, perhaps even fragile. They still have Classical characteristics. The backs are square and the top sometimes wide and curving to fit to the shape of the sitter, though Sheraton did design some shield backs as they were still popular. The seats are over-stuffed, and the legs square-tapered or delicately turned, sometimes forward splaying. Carving has disappeared and has been replaced by inlay work, or painted designs.

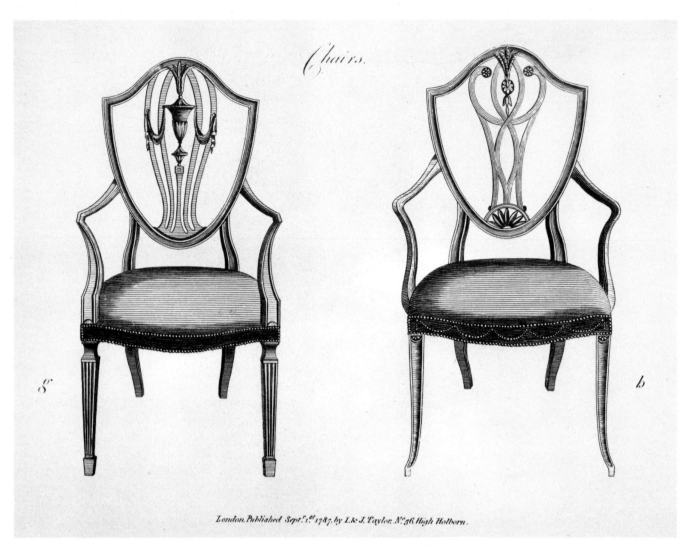

Chairs.

London. Published Sept.r 1.st 1787, by I. & J. Taylor, N.o 56. High Holborn.

23

22
Design for two shield-back armchairs by George Hepplewhite, from his *Cabinet-Maker and Upholsterer's Guide.*

23
Set of six upright chairs made by Thomas Chippendale. Victoria and Albert Museum.

24
Six upright chair designs by Thomas Sheraton, from his *Cabinet-Maker's and Upholsterer's Drawing-Book.* Strong Classical influence can clearly be seen.

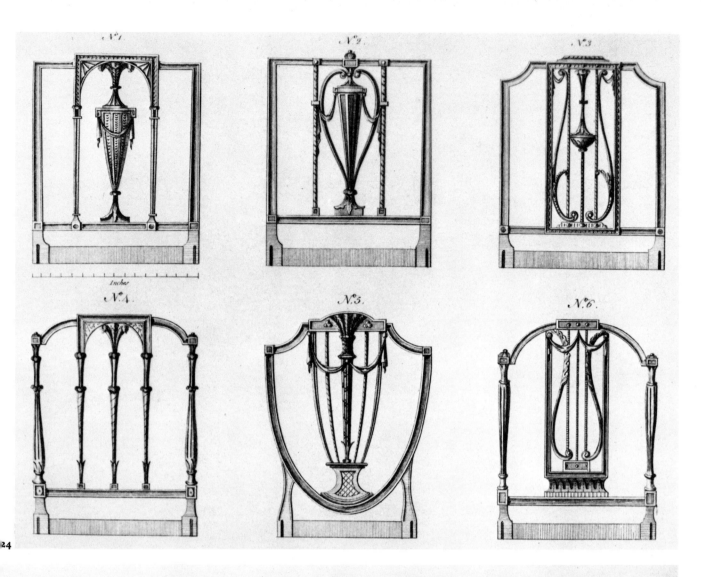

25
A late 18th-century English stick-back 'Windsor' chair in yew, with oak seat.

Sets of six chairs in the Hepplewhite or Sheraton style, including one or two chairs with arms, were made in the first years of the 19th century. Their price in the salerooms depends upon the design, the carving if any, the quality of painting or inlay, and the number of dealers interested in buying them at any sale. Single chairs of the same period can still be found in Britain for as little as £10, or £40 a pair. If you cannot afford a full set why not collect a harlequin set, as so many people have been doing for some years now? A harlequin set comprises six or eight chairs of one basic style, but each slightly different and bought separately as a single piece. Many years ago I built up a collection of eight mahogany 18th- or early 19th-century dining chairs which had two major features in common: they all had square and straight legs with chamfered inner edges, and splat backs in the Chippendale manner. This type of collecting is becoming more difficult largely because dealers are buying up the ones and twos and using them as 'quarries' for replacement parts for similar chairs. But you can still make up an attractive harlequin set and add to its attractiveness by re-

covering all the seats in the same material.

Once Chippendale's designs had become well known – his book ran to three editions – a host of provincial and country cabinet-makers and craftsmen began to imitate them. They produced considerable quantities of chairs, the designs quite often differing from the originals, and thus originated what is now widely referred to as 'Country Chippendale' chairs. The master had of course advocated the use of mahogany, a wood which lends itself beautifully to carving and which has a fine grain. His imitators, however, generally used a host of inferior woods, usually those grown naturally in England, such as elm, fruitwood, beech, tulipwood and deal. Some 'Country Chippendale' chairs have all the characteristics but few of the graces of real Chippendale. They can be thick, unevenly cut and planed, and badly jointed, and have solid wooden seats. Little wonder, then, that I managed to get one at a house sale in Yorkshire in 1960 for only ten shillings ($1.20) and yet I rate it as one of my best 'friends' among my collection. An interesting set could therefore be made up at a modest outlay. A great majority of dining chairs

26
Country Chippendale armchair in elm, with wooden seat. The splat is typical of the Chippendale style. Note the rough proportions of the chair. Author's Collection.

marked '18th century' or '*c.* 1810' in dealers' shops throughout the country are specimens made by country craftsmen.

One of the most popular dining-chair styles, however, was the Trafalgar chair. This was a product of the Regency period, and it reached the height of its development in the years 1805–10, the former year being the date of Nelson's great victory. The Trafalgar chair is immediately recognisable by its sabre-shaped legs, front and back, and its rope rail back. In design the chair resembles the ancient Greek *klismos*. A great many of these chairs were made by a firm which called its factory the Trafalgar Works, after the victory. The style is graceful and flowing. The cane seating was sometimes replaced by a drop-in covered seat. As a style the Trafalgar chair has remained popular and has been copied more widely than any other.

Trafalgar chairs were made in beechwood, and then painted black. They were also made of mahogany and, occasionally, even of rosewood. The beechwood chairs were sometimes stained so that at first sight the wood looks like rosewood, the grains being similar. Such a

chair might well be described in a sale catalogue as 'simulated rosewood'.

Another piece of dining-room furniture is the dining table. In the 17th century these were usually solid oak pieces called refectory tables, rectangular in shape and standing either on a pair of bulbous legs running into flat bases, or on four turned legs with stretchers between the four legs. In the 18th century, when mahogany came into widespread use for furniture, the first dining tables were heavy, and were supported on four cabriole-type legs, without stretchers. The designs were then developed. There might be two 'D' ends on four legs each, with contraptions allowing the insertion of additional leaves for extending the table. The flaps might have their own gate-legged arrangement. Then, by the end of the century, large circular tables were made, mounted on strong central pedestals. This type of table gave the cabinet-maker the opportunity to produce a fine, large surface of one whole piece of figured wood, such as rosewood. The edge on the top might be inlaid in brass or coloured wood, or even ivory, and a 2 or 3 inch apron of curved wood fitted just under the top.

27
Sheraton-style mahogany Carlton House table of the end of the 18th century.

28
'Trafalgar' upright chair of about 1806, with cane seat and rope motifs on the back. Royal Pavilion, Brighton.

29
Hepplewhite-style sideboard of the late 18th century on square chamfered tapering legs.

30
Very early 16th-century oak chest, with linen-fold decoration on the front panels. Copies of this type of chest made in the 17th century can quite often be found in country antique shops.

31
English refectory table on bulb supports. Late 16th-century.

Another contemporary table was the gate-legged version, with four legs, usually turned and sometimes with pad feet. Two of the legs moved outwards to ninety degrees to support two flaps hinged to the central panel.

The dining room also had a sideboard after about 1765. This is a largish piece of furniture mainly for holding food dishes during mealtimes. Hepplewhite designed some very elegant ones, which were copied by some excellent craftsmen. Sideboards vary in appointments. You may find one with three drawers under the top and, in addition, two cupboards underneath the drawers. Sideboards may be bow-fronted, straight-fronted, and serpentine-fronted. Sometimes they are even break-fronted. Generally they are on square, tapering legs or on turned legs, and sometimes they are inlaid.

Since you spend a third of your life in bed, you will want to have the bedroom attractively furnished. At the same time it ought perhaps to be sparsely furnished because pieces collect dust, and you can limit the furniture to articles you really need, such as a bed, a pair of upright chairs (country-style Sheraton will do here), a dressing table, a tallboy or chest of drawers, a clothes press or wardrobe, and two side tables.

Unless you particularly want a four-poster bed (and they collect dust in large quantities on the cornice), a modern bed will not spoil a room otherwise filled with antique pieces, since it will be totally covered with a bedspread. A four-poster, by the way, whether in oak of the 17th or 18th century or mahogany of the late 18th or early 19th century, can generally be obtained for a reasonable price.

The chest of drawers was, in 18th-century England, almost as important as was the commode in France, except that chests did not figure as importantly in English drawing rooms. Chests came in a variety of shapes and sizes and in several woods: walnut in the early 18th century, mahogany, sometimes satinwood,

and then even pinewood in the later part of the century. An enormous range of chests, both town and country varieties, is still available to lovers of antiques. Country chests are usually of deal, veneered on the front surfaces in mahogany, the better ones also veneered on the sides. Sometimes a chest is in oak, with mahogany banding on the drawers. The lovely figured walnut chests of the William and Mary and Queen Anne periods, often banded in walnut of different grain, can fetch high prices today, but they are well worth it, as some experts consider the Age of Walnut (c. 1670–c. 1740) the finest period of English furniture.

The mahogany chests of the mid and late 18th century came in several forms. They were straight-fronted with straight bracket feet or splayed bracket feet; or bow-fronted with splayed bracket feet; or serpentine-fronted with the same feet or occasionally with ogee feet. They had three long drawers; or three long and two short; or four long and two short; or four long; or two long and four short. Some were inlaid round the edge of the top and on the drawer fronts. A good specimen had matching drawer fronts, that is, the

wood came from the same tree and was cut so that each front had the same grain configuration.

An enormous number of country chests were made. When looking at chests watch for worm-holes. If the piece is solid mahogany, there should be none. But if it is veneered with mahogany, worms can get through the veneer, having come through the deal or oak part first. A veneered chest should cost much less than a solid mahogany one.

Another popular chest of drawers is the stripped pine type. They are often small, with two long and two short drawers. They were generally painted when first made in the late 18th century, and they have been stripped in recent years, as there is a vogue for stripped pine furniture. Several shops in London specialise in it. You can still get a small chest of this kind cheaply in the country. It will probably have been fitted with bogus brass handles, which is really wrong, for the originals will have had turned wooden knobs.

The chest may not be enough for your needs and you could buy a tallboy instead (or in addition, if the bedroom is large enough). The tallboy is a chest of drawers

32

32
One of the finest surviving commodes of the Louis XV period.
It was made by Gaudreaux in about 1740, in kingwood and
mahogany veneer on oak, with gilt-bronze mounts. Wallace
Collection, London.

33
Very fine example of the American mid 18th-century high
chest of drawers. It is basically in the Queen Anne style of Boston
and has been lacquered. H. F. du Pont Winterthur Museum,
Delaware.

34
Hepplewhite-style bow-front chest of drawers of the end of the 18th century. The wooden knobs have replaced earlier brass handles.

35
A late 18th-century American washstand. The top supports are reeded and carved. American Museum in Britain, Claverton Manor, Bath.

on a chest of drawers. The earliest ones were of walnut and were made at the turn of the 18th century. The lower half sometimes has only two drawers, mounted on long cabriole legs, the upper part having three or four long and two or three short drawers, surmounted by a moulded cornice, or even a broken pediment in the Baroque manner. The walnut is usually figured and sometimes banded round the edges. These are sometimes called chests on stands. Later came the extra drawer or drawers in the bottom half, mounted now on short squat legs, bun feet or bracket feet.

Walnut tallboys were superseded by mahogany ones in a range of sizes and with variegated decoration. They were as high as 7 feet 6 inches and as wide as 4 feet. Good 18th-century tallboys in the Chippendale manner are not common. One fetched £350 (about $840) in 1968. Copies made in the 19th century could be found for much less, but they might be the largest size, which will not suit all bedrooms.

The tallboy's relative, the clothes press, is a useful piece of furniture. This arrived in about the middle of the 18th century. The bottom half had two long, or two long and two short drawers, or three long and two short, and the top half was a cupboard of two doors. Surmounting the cupboard was a pediment of varying designs. The principal feature of the doors was that the panels matched, that is, they were cut from the same tree. Sometimes above the doors was a frieze with decoration, such as fretwork moulding. A clothes press will generally take all hanging clothes except long dresses and overcoats.

36
Extremely fine mahogany sofa, probably made by Samuel McIntire, the celebrated American craftsman. Museum of Fine Arts, Boston, Massachusetts; M. & M. Karolik Collection.

37
American mahogany card table on pedestal base with splay feet, probably made by Duncan Phyfe in about 1800. American Museum in Britain, Claverton Manor, Bath.

A few words should be said about the oak and fruit-wood furniture which can still be obtained in most shops and salerooms, especially in country towns. Gate-legged dining tables, side tables with barley-sugar legs and one drawer under the top, dressing tables with two side drawers almost square in shape interspersed by a rectangular drawer, and round tables on centre pedestals and three splayed feet can all be found and bought cheaply. Much of this furniture will be 19th-century, or at best, late 18th-century, for the country craftsmen continued making the various styles long after they were superseded or abandoned by town craftsmen.

The Welsh made considerable quantities of furniture in oak, elm, fruitwood and ash, and much of it was strongly national in style. Few Welsh craftsmen concerned themselves with English styles or with mahogany, rosewood or the other exotic woods until the 19th century. Two pieces in particular are sought, the Welsh dresser and a kind of cupboard called the *cwpwrdd* **15** *tridarn*.

The dresser is in two parts, the bottom half of which

37

either has two cupboards, over which are two or three drawers in a row, or has only the drawer line, supported by square legs. The top half consists of a row of shelves, usually three or four, ranging from shallow to deep in descending order. The earlier dressers had no backboards at all, for the piece was affixed to the wall.

The *cwpwrdd tridarn* is a three-stage piece of furniture, in oak or elm. The two lower parts are cupboards, the higher tier being set back a few inches from the lower. The third tier was a space at the top covered by a moulded cornice on turned pillar supports. The back was boarded. A *cwpwrdd tridarn* generally costs as much as an 18th-century dresser, for though not so elegant it is harder to find. The best were made in Anglesey.

American antique furniture is rich and vigorous, and much of it is original in design. Naturally, many of the styles resembled British and, after the War of Independence, European styles, but even these adaptations had peculiarly native characteristics. Moreover, American furniture was, on the whole, extremely well made. It is

a splendid field for collecting, although an expensive one, and to start presents a formidable challenge to the ingenuity of collectors in Britain and elsewhere, since few good pieces are found in shops or the ordinary salerooms.

American craftsmen made more or less the same sort of pieces as the British, but they also developed their own ideas. Many adaptations of British styles are regarded now by an increasing number of experts as better in quality than the models from which they derive. These adaptations followed styles prevalent in Britain, but there was a gap of about a generation. American Queen Anne furniture, for example, lasted well into the middle of the 18th century, and in some instances the newer developments of the earlier Georgian period in Britain were incorporated into pieces made by American craftsmen. A splendid example of American Queen Anne furniture is a high chest of drawers on a stand, sometimes called a highboy, 33 illustrated in this book. It was made in Boston in the decade 1740–50. The carved shell motif is a typical

American adornment of the time, but the imitation oriental lacquer in this case is the exception rather than the rule. American pieces were more usually simple in decoration, with the emphasis on the selection of wood grain and the skilful use of veneers.

36

It is difficult to give a price for a highboy. Many were made – and made most beautifully – but they are still much sought after, and to some extent it will depend upon the skill of joinery and craftsmanship. The lowest price you might pay for a good highboy in the United States would be about $500 (about £208).

In the 1760s Chippendale designs, already dominating British furniture, reached America and were an immediate success. But American craftsmen did not copy them slavishly: they elaborated freely on the basic ideas. The term 'Chippendale' furniture has a much wider significance in American furniture than it has in British furniture. Much of it is not in line with British contemporary work. Smaller chests of drawers in the Chippendale style, for example, differed from typical British ones in such features as heavy shell decoration across the top or the bottom drawers. The chests often had block fronts, a very American conception, where the middle of the chest recedes in a kind of flattened arc, and the ends protrude in a bulge of the same geometric shape as the middle part. Such a chest, in cherrywood, could be expensive, but might cost less if a country piece with less refinement of detail and finish.

35

American Hepplewhite styles were fashionable from about 1790 to the turn of the century, and were followed by American Sheraton, along with American Directoire and Empire ideas from France. Typical Hepplewhite features were thin legs on chairs and small tables, and fine and subtle decoration of the flat surfaces, using inlay or carefully graded grain. The tambour door was adapted in a number of pieces as a most elegant feature in such pieces as washstands, desks and cupboards.

The Hepplewhite, Sheraton and French styles were sometimes mingled, and a 'school' of furniture of this kind prevailed in the early years of the 19th century. This is sometimes called the 'Federal Style'. One of the cabinet-makers who specialised in it was Duncan Phyfe (1768–1854), a Scottish emigrant who set up a business in New York and made some of the finest American furniture of the period. He made sofas – some of these have grandeur and elegance – chairs in the Hepplewhite and Sheraton manner, sideboards, pier tables, and secretaire bookcases, among other pieces, and his work is in great demand. How many he himself had a hand in we shall never know, but it is said that about a hundred craftsmen at one time worked for him. There are consequently a number of pieces available, but at a high price, even for a simple card table.

13

37

Looking back a little, some original American pieces of the 17th century are of great interest. The first immigrants who arrived in the 'Mayflower' were relatively poor, and they had little but the clothes they stood in. They brought few pieces of furniture, probably only those which were strictly functional, such as chairs. Much furniture therefore had to be made by themselves, and at first it was crude, like the country furniture made in Britain. But it seems it was well constructed, for it had to last for a long time.

The Colonists made the usual pieces, such as gate-legged tables, press cupboards, chests and chairs, with and without arms. A particularly interesting type of chair was the 'Dutch' armchair with turned posts and spindles. There were two kinds: the Brewster, which had two rows of four spindles in the back between horizontal rails, and another row under a horizontal arm, on each side, and the Carver which had three spindles between the horizontal rails. Both chairs were generally made of ash or maple, and they had rush seating. The Brewster was named after one of the immigrants in the 'Mayflower' who, it is said, brought such a chair with him from England, while the Carver was named after the first governor of the colony set up by the Pilgrim Fathers from the 'Mayflower' and succeeding ships, who is also believed to have brought one with him from home.

38

American craftsmen also made Windsor stick-back chairs. These had thick, solid wood, saddle-shaped seats on four turned, spindle legs, which were positioned at a rake angle and sometimes strengthened by a stretcher arrangement. From the top of the seat, at carefully calculated positions, more spindles projected upwards, slanting backwards, to form a curve, and held in position by a top rail. These were first made in America in about 1720, in Philadelphia. Over the years they acquired additions of style, such as ball feet, and in the 19th century craftsmen began to mount them on rockers. These were the forerunners of the rocking chairs which are part of American 19th-century folklore. The best Windsor-type chairs were made of hardwood and had nine or more spindles.

2

America has had its own kind of country furniture, especially in the early 19th century. New England pieces were generally made in pine or maple or cherry. Some of the furniture reflected the origins of the regions; for example, in pieces from the Hudson valley, where the Dutch had settled, many Dutch styles persisted. One article which is much sought and is expensive is a two-door cupboard on huge bun feet. It is called a *kas*, and the doors are often decorated with a type of inlay known as *trompe l'oeil*, which has a three-dimensional aspect.

38
American Carver chair of ash, made in about 1670. American Museum in Britain, Claverton Manor, Bath.

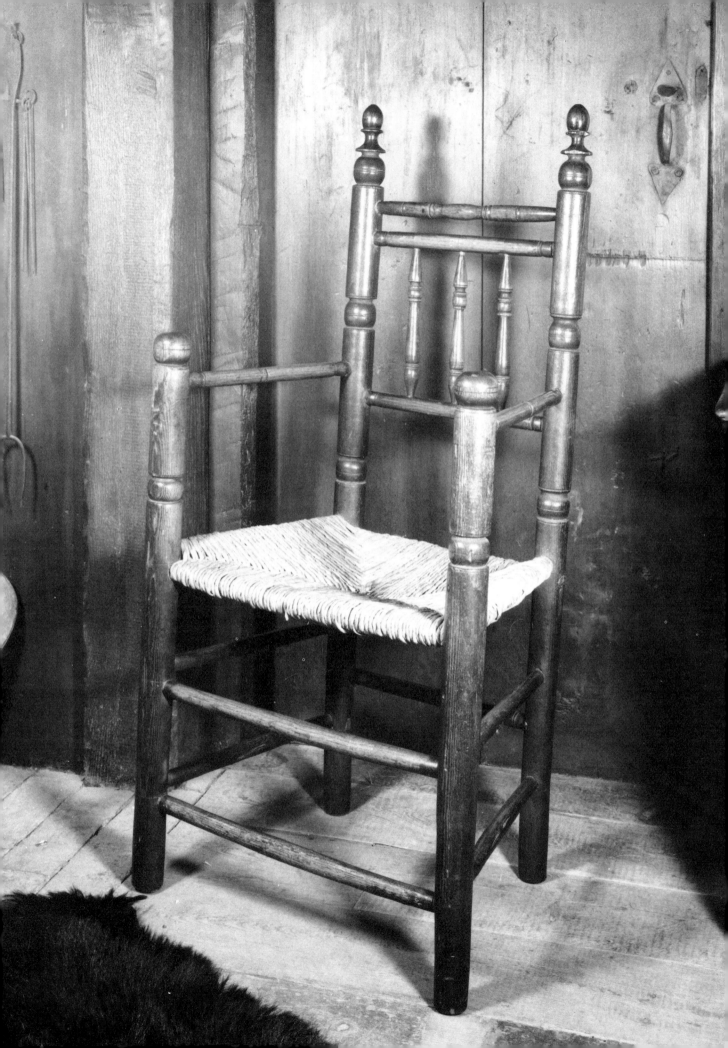

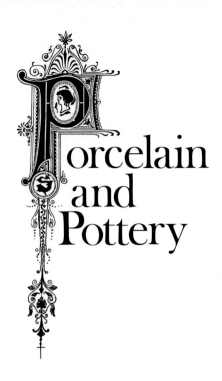

Porcelain and Pottery

Old porcelain and pottery are among the most decorative antiques that you can buy. Some articles can cost a considerable amount, like the pair of Meissen figures sold by Christie's in October 1969 for £25,365 (about $60,876); others can be picked up for very little, though the cheapest variety is becoming harder to find. If you decide to collect porcelain, whatever budget you have to work to, a splendid variety of articles has been made over the centuries in many countries, and since they are part of the social history of the world, they must in the end appreciate in value.

In the Victorian era there was a great upsurge in the manufacture of pottery and porcelain. Some of it was original in design, and although not always attractive, it was often gay and arresting. Some of it was reproduction, well done and occasionally difficult to distinguish from the original. But as it is not yet classed as antique, it is beyond the scope of this book, although you can read about it in one of the books mentioned in the bibliography.

Antique porcelain tends to be more expensive than pottery, with a few exceptions like very early Wedgwood or Whieldon. This is because less of it was made and it is a finer product in so many ways. It is translucent, except for the very heavy type. Pieces are generally lighter and thinner, and the decoration is usually of better quality. Cups and bowls, and similar pieces, have a resonant ring about them, rather like good glass. A good deal of porcelain was made to order by the best potters available, often in sets such as tableware, in much the same way as furniture might be ordered from, for instance, Chippendale or Gillow.

There are two basic types of porcelain, soft-paste and hard-paste. Hard-paste is usually called 'true porcelain'. It is made from china clay and china stone. The article is shaped in the clay and it is then rendered into a glass-like condition by the china stone with the application of heat. Glazing is done at the same time. If you should be unlucky enough to break a piece of hard-paste porcelain, the edges of the two or more fragments would feel smooth and glossy. But you can determine hard-paste without going to this extreme by looking for a bare unglazed spot on the base and feeling if it is hard. Porcelain from China was hard-paste, and so was the best of the 18th-century continental European manufacture. But in England in the first years of that century only three factories are recorded as having made it: Plymouth, Bristol and New Hall.

Soft-paste porcelain was little more than a reproduction of hard-paste, the constituents being different. It was made of clay and glass, but the glazing of the surface was done afterwards as a separate operation. Soft-

39
Early 18th-century Chinese 'pilgrim-flask' vase of porcelain in *famille rose* decoration. Percival David Foundation, London University.

40
Chinese *famille verte* plate about 2 feet in diameter. *Famille verte* was one of the most popular of the Chinese decorative patterns on porcelain pieces of the K'ang Hsi period (1662–1772) in the early days of the Manchus. Ascott Collection, National Trust.

41
A Chinese blue-green, white-glazed porcelain ewer of the Sung Dynasty, and dating from about the 11th century. Seligman Collection, Arts Council of Great Britain.

42
Beautiful hard-paste figure of a heron made by J. J. Kändler of Meissen in about 1731. Pflueger Collection, New York.

paste porcelain fragments have rough surfaces and a slippery feel about them. You can scratch soft-paste quite easily with a sharp point.

A third kind of porcelain is bone china, introduced in about 1794 in England by Josiah Spode (1733–96). This was almost, but not quite, a hard-paste porcelain, and it was made by including a large quantity of bone ash in the mixture prior to firing. The result was a fine, translucent product which has set a standard for bone china manufacture ever since. It was invented chiefly because of the passing of an Act of Parliament prohibiting the purchase of foreign porcelain, then at the height of fashion. This was one of William Pitt's measures to conserve the economy of Britain in order to be able to prosecute the war against France. Bone china is very rarely found outside Britain.

Porcelain was invented by the Chinese potters in the time of the T'ang dynasty, as long ago as the 8th century. They fused china clay (kaolin) and china

40

stone at very high temperatures and produced a fine, white, translucent porcelain. The Sung dynasty, which followed the T'ang, witnessed great improvements in technique and quality, including the use of blue as a colour for decoration. Under the Ming emperors, who succeeded the Sung, brilliant colours – reds, yellows and turquoise – were introduced along with exotic patterns, including fine birds, figures of animals, such as dragons, and delightful landscapes. When the Manchus crushed the Mings in the middle of the 17th century, China was exporting porcelain to Europe in large quantities, and the principal styles, specially made, were *famille rose*, *famille verte*, and two other not so common patterns, *famille noire* and *famille jaune*. *Famille rose* is decorated with its colour on the glaze in rose pink.

Pieces of 18th-century Chinese porcelain can be bought today, and they include plates, vases – in pairs or sets – cups and saucers; sometimes they have European designs especially for export to Europe.

But this fine Chinese porcelain was not cheap to buy in Europe, and for many years European chemists and potters searched for the secret of hard-paste porcelain-making. Then, in 1708, a German chemist of Meissen, Johann Böttger (1682–1719) re-discovered the use of kaolin for making white porcelain and, two years later Augustus, the Elector of Saxony, set up a factory there. Böttger then began to produce splendid pieces which became the envy of Europe, for the secret was not to be shared with any other factory for some time. He made figures, and he also made pieces modelled on silverware of the time, such as coffee pots. After about 1720 Meissen introduced marks for porcelain, which were inscribed on the base. The commonest was the crossed swords motif.

Two fine craftsmen who worked at Meissen were J. G. Kirchner and J. J. Kändler, who also made figures, and these have become among the most famous in porcelain history. The Meissen factory was taken

45

46

43 *(page 54)*
Staffordshire salt-glaze mug, enamelled in colours, of about 1755.
Fitzwilliam Museum, Cambridge.

44 *(page 55)*
The Goatherd, a fine piece of Bristol hard-paste porcelain, of
about 1775. Fenton House, London.

45
Very fine, Swansea soft-paste porcelain dish, of about 1820.
Swansea and Nantgarw porcelain by Billingsley was among the
best ever made in Britain in the 19th century. Victoria and
Albert Museum, London.

46
Sèvres soft-paste porcelain breakfast tray with appurtenances.
It was made in about 1770, and is decorated in polychrome and
gold. Musée National Céramique, Sèvres.

47
Two Chelsea porcelain figures of about 1755: (right) *Painting*,
and (left) *Astronomy*. Victoria and Albert Museum, London.

over in the Seven Years War (1756–63) by Frederick
the Great, who had the best pieces, the moulds and the
most useful apparatus shipped to his palace at Potsdam.
Meissen porcelain was never the same after this. Good
pieces were made, especially when the original works
were under the management of Count Marcolini, from
1774 to 1814, but after that the products became
decidedly inferior. They were mainly imitations of the
originals and they are referred to now as Dresden
pieces (Meissen was near Dresden). Meissen pieces are
now extremely expensive, but Dresden is still obtainable at a reasonable price.

In France, potters were also looking for ways to
manufacture hard-paste porcelain, as the Meissen
products were becoming too expensive even for the
carefree aristocrats of the entourage of Louis XV. In
about 1759 a soft-paste porcelain business, founded at
Vincennes in 1738 and removed to Sèvres in 1756, was **59**
bought by the king, and thereafter the Sèvres factory
made the bulk of good French porcelain up to the **8**
Revolution of 1789. In 1769 potters finally discovered
the art of making hard-paste porcelain, and all kinds of
most beautiful pieces were made. Blue and pink were **46**
the principal colours, and at Sèvres the idea of plaques,

47

that is, pictures within frames of gilt, on rectangular, square, or other shaped panels of porcelain, was developed, and the plaques adorned furniture, clocks and ornaments. They were often signed by the makers.

Research into the manufacture of hard-paste porcelain was also pursued in Britain, and in 1768 William Cookworthy produced a hard-paste porcelain at the Plymouth pottery. Two years later the business was transferred to Bristol, and in 1781 it moved again to New Hall. These were the only factories which made hard-paste porcelain in Britain in the 18th century. For the rest, soft-paste porcelain had already been produced at a number of places, and although it was not as good as hard-paste, it was nonetheless fine and was in some demand. Factories making soft-paste porcelain included Bow, Chelsea, Coalport, Derby, Lowestoft, Minton, Nantgarw, Rockingham, Spode and Worcester.

Bow porcelain was first made in 1745. It was heavy and not very translucent. Although tableware was made, Bow is best known for figures. Chelsea porcelain was made for about 27 years only, from 1743 until about 1770. Founded by Huguenot refugees, the Chelsea works passed into the hands of Nicholas Sprimont, who sold it to the Derby business. Chelsea made soft-paste porcelain and copied Meissen styles. Sprimont experimented with bone ash as a constituent in the hope of attaining a hard-paste porcelain, but he never achieved the quality later enjoyed by the Spode business. After the take-over by Derby, porcelain made by Derby was decorated for some time at Chelsea, but the old Chelsea styles did not survive. This type of porcelain is called Chelsea-Derby or Derby-Chelsea. A real Chelsea plate can cost a considerable amount, and the Chelsea-Derby figures, which are not regarded as good as the Chelsea ones, still fetch large sums, even when slightly damaged.

Coalport porcelain was made in great quantities and much of it can still be bought in antique shops today, although, of course, sets of dinner services cannot be found so easily. The Coalport factory was founded in about 1795 by John Rose, who had once worked at the Caughley factory and who took it over in 1800 and ran it as a separate business until 1814. Rose employed, among others, the services of the distinguished china-painter, William Billingsley, who had worked at Nantgarw and had discovered how to make a very white porcelain. Coalport porcelain of the early 19th century had bright colours and floral patterns of roses, and Meissen and Sèvres tablewares were both imitated and deliberately copied. You can still find a good Coalport single plate of the early 19th century for a small sum of money.

Derby porcelain is very famous, and interest in the old styles has been greatly enhanced in recent years by the exceedingly good reproductions of these styles

48

49

48
Wedgwood creamware tea pot of about 1770. Donald Towner Collection.

49
Wedgwood jasperware vase, a late 18th-century copy of a Greek vase in the British Museum. Wedgwood Museum, Staffordshire.

50
Porcelain cup and saucer in blue, gilt and white, made in about 1800 in the Worcester factory under the direction of Flight and Barr. Author's Collection.

produced by the Derby works. From the middle of the 18th century Derby began to make figures. Then, under William Duesbury, who became sole owner in 1779, the factory began to produce a great variety of porcelain, including good copies of Meissen and Sèvres ware and a fair range of quite original pieces. This household ware was characterised by flowers, scrolls, elaborate designs, Chinese landscapes and lattice borders. After 1784, much of it was marked with a crown over a pair of crossed batons and a capital 'D'. The mark varied in colour up to the end of the century, when it was reddish. Old Derby porcelain is not cheap: a Meissen-type figure of an Italian Harlequin fetched 100 guineas (about $252) at a sale in 1967 and I saw a simple tea bowl and saucer, marked as pre-1880 and priced at £70 (about $168), in a well-known shop in London.

From about 1757 to 1802 the Lowestoft factory produced soft-paste porcelain chiefly in blue and white. Pieces are occasionally dated, such as tea caddies, jugs and plaques, and the designs are predominantly oriental. Many people collect Lowestoft, even though it is not very fine and usually rather expensive.

A busy porcelain manufacturer of the first years of the 19th century was Thomas Minton. He concentrated on tableware, dinner, dessert and tea services, often with a dark blue background, filled with flowers, and sometimes Chinese landscape motifs. Minton is still made, some of it in the old styles.

Some of the very best early 19th-century soft-paste porcelain in Britain was made at Nantgarw in Wales. A factory was set up in 1813 by William Billingsley, and over the next nine years exquisite designs were produced on the finest white porcelain. There is very little of it left now, and a single plate, with floral pattern – Nantgarw flowers are most beautifully painted – fetched over £150 (about $360) at a sale in 1967. If you should ever come across any Nantgarw, even if damaged, you should buy it, for its exceptional translucency and its excellent decoration single it out even among pieces made by the best of the British porcelain-makers. In 1822 the Nantgarw factory was absorbed by Coalport, and thereafter its individuality vanished.

Rockingham is a good aristocratic-sounding name for china, and it has to be admitted that even the rather inferior earthenware made by this firm has grandeur. Porcelain, however, was made by Rockingham for only about twenty years, from around 1820. Even these pieces were extravagantly designed and made with masses of gilt, odd shapes to plates, and Rococo-type lids to tea pots and sugar bowls. Dinner and dessert services were often made to order, marked with the gryphon crest of the Marquis of Rockingham, on whose land the factory had been erected. Rockingham is difficult to find in complete sets; a good tea service will cost a good deal of money, but single pieces do turn up in Britain for only a few pounds.

At the turn of the 19th century, Josiah Spode (1754–1827) invented feldspar porcelain. This was not unlike hard-paste, and it was the result of mixing china clay, china stone, bone ash and feldspar (aluminium silicate). It was an instant success, in an age when European hard-paste porcelain was still difficult to come by, because of import restrictions. A vast range of pieces was made in all kinds of colours – green, dark blue, yellow and red – and the decorations included fruit, flowers, animal patterns, and landscapes. Some landscapes were scenes from ancient Rome as depicted by Piranesi, the Italian engraver, and his school. A considerable number of pieces were made in deep blue, a style that continued after 1827, when Spode's son had died and the business had been bought by Copeland. Many pieces of this time are marked 'Copeland Spode', and while they may not all be valuable just now, they are well worth collecting, because they are bound to become collectors' pieces before long.

The last of the great names in porcelain in Britain is Worcester. The Worcester Porcelain Company began in about 1750, and the earliest pieces, for about thirty years, are associated with Dr Wall, who was a founding partner of the firm. From the very beginning the Worcester factory experimented boldly with decoration and colour, using yellow, apple-green, powder-blue, deep red and purple grounds, with thin glazing, and executing landscapes, fine floral patterns, imagery, gilt lattice-work, or similar patterns.

51

52

51
Dutch Delftware (tin-glazed earthenware) plate, painted in blue, of about 1670. Victoria and Albert Museum, London.

52
Leeds basket, in blue willow pattern, of about 1815.

53
The Sailor's Farewell, one of a pair of Staffordshire figures of about 1810. The other is *The Sailor's Return*.

In 1783 the firm was purchased by Thomas Flight and presented to his sons, Joseph and John. For six years the china, in most cases, was marked with the name 'Flight' in blue, and from 1789 to 1792 with 'Flight' in red. In that latter year, Martin Barr joined Joseph Flight (John had died), and up to 1807 Worcester ware was marked with the words 'Flight and Barr' under a sort of crown, or with simply a 'B' for Barr. From 1807 to 1813, when Barr's son joined the firm, the mark 'BFB' was incised under a crown, and from 1813 to 1840, 'FBB'. Other marks also appeared, especially, in 1820, a mark comprising a 'B' with a reversed small 'C' at the left of the 'B'.

Worcester is characterised by the high quality of the work, the glaze and the decoration. Its exotic patterns (birds, foliage, gilding in fret motif, figures, shapes) and its sharp colours, especially the blue, have made it one of the most collectable types of china in the British porcelain tradition. You could find an 'FBB' plate for a modest sum, and a cup and saucer marked 'B' (1800) for even less. But early Worcester is expensive, and a single plate with birds on a blue background, of the Dr Wall period, fetched £130 (about $312) at a sale in 1968.

Pottery is a much wider field for collection, and it is not possible to do more than give it a cursory glance in this book. It has been made for at least 6,000 years, but today, except for the early types and one or two particularly fine makes, such as Wedgwood and Whieldon, it is on the whole cheaper to buy. For two centuries it has been called the poor man's porcelain, for potters have reproduced, in earthenware and glaze, a considerable range of porcelain styles, shapes and colours.

One of the best imitations of porcelain was tin-glazed earthenware. It appears to have been made first in England at Norwich in the 16th century, but it has been named 'English delftware', after the town in Holland which, in the late 17th century, became a well-known centre for tin-glaze ware. Delftware was also made at Lambeth in London, in Bristol, in Glasgow, and in Dublin. It is notable for its designs in deep blue, which are underneath the glaze, and they often have a very pale appearance. The principal decoration took the form of landscapes, family scenes and flowers in the European or Chinese style, and these were sometimes painted on tiles in sets, to make up the surround to a fireplace.

English delftware is more widely collected every year. Typical articles are jugs, bowls, plates, vases, cups and saucers. A 17th-century, Bristol-made, Delft plate obtained £25 (about $60) at a sale in 1968, but I have seen English delftware of the same century for less.

A particularly attractive ware to collect is Leeds pottery. This factory started to make tableware and figures in the middle of the 18th century, and these articles are remarkable for their rich, creamy white colour and their fine glaze. One feature generally associated with Leeds and which appears in many pieces made there is basket-work, pierced interlaced reeds which are good representations of the water plant. Another feature is lattice-work of twigging as edging to plates, though this is not confined to Leeds. Leeds articles are often astonishingly light in weight for their size.

Staffordshire pottery is, of course, almost a household name, but it is a term and not a product of one factory, for at the end of the 18th century, well over twenty factories were producing considerable quantities of gaily decorated and, on the whole, quite well-made tableware, ornaments and figures. A pioneer in this field was Thomas Whieldon (1719-95), whose wares are now fetching very high prices. He set up in business in about 1740 and was to become a dominating influence on British pottery. His earthenware was remarkable for the galaxy of colours he used, achieved by different coloured clays and also by staining the glazing. Although he made a variety of tableware distinctive by its simplicity of shape, he is perhaps better known for figures of human beings, real or imaginary, and of animals, and for Toby jugs. He made much salt-glaze

43 ware. This is a stoneware in which the glazing is achieved by adding salt during the firing at a very high temperature, and the result, at first glance, is not unlike porcelain, for which it was intended to be a substitute. Articles which have applied reliefs and mouldings are quite attractive, especially if they are in two or more colours.

It is probable that Whieldon began the vogue for the stoneware figures' which have been associated with Staffordshire potteries ever since. A real Whieldon Toby jug would cost quite a high sum of money, but good 19th-century copies cost much less.

Even the most cursory review of pottery would be woefully lacking if it did not include mention of Wedgwood ware. Josiah Wedgwood (1730–95) worked for some time with Whieldon. In about 1760 he set up his own business with the aim of producing earthenware as much like porcelain as he could make it. He wanted to do better than salt-glaze. One result was his cream-

48 coloured ware, which became known as Queen's ware because he made a service for George III's wife, Queen Charlotte, and she liked it. This creamware was extremely successful, and Wedgwood became rich. But he did not stop trying to improve his products, and in

54 1774 he introduced his celebrated 'jasperware'. This was made by mixing clay with large amounts of barytes and barium carbonate; the result was a stoneware hard enough to be wheel-polished. At first the colouring agents were mixed with the clay and chemicals, and the colours used were blue, green, black and lilac, but afterwards the articles were coloured only on the surface. As a rule pieces were two-toned, that is, they had white reliefs or moulds on the colour background. Blue was the most common colour.

One of Wedgwood's brightest business ideas was to

49 profit by the revival of interest in Classical things, stimulated throughout Europe by the discoveries at

54

55

54
Wedgwood jasperware plaque, white on pale blue, of about 1780. The figure is that of Sir Eyre Coote. British Museum, London.

55
English delftware wall pocket made in Liverpool in about 1760. City of Liverpool Museums.

56
Pitcher made by W. E. Tucker of Philadelphia in about 1828; a fine example of American porcelain. Newark Museum, U.S.A.

57

58

Pompeii and made fashionable in Britain by Robert Adam, the architect and interior designer. Wedgwood created a whole new style of pottery which was called 'Etruria', from the name he gave to his works because it was to produce copies of old Etruscan and Roman-type pottery, such as vases, urns, plaques, cameos and ewers, as well as tableware and household ornaments. One piece he reproduced was the Portland Vase. This celebrated glass-cameo vase, said to have been made in Roman Egypt in the days of Julius Caesar, turned up in Italy in the 17th century. In 1770 Sir William Hamilton, husband of Nelson's Emma, bought it and then sold it to the Duchess of Portland. It was by then a celebrated relic, and it became much better known when Wedgwood copied it in jasper some time towards the end of the decade 1780–90. Thirty copies were made at first, and it then ran into several 'editions'. In 1845, a lunatic got into the British Museum while the vase was on show and smashed it. It was restored only because someone was able to lend the restorer one of Wedgwood's first jasper copies. In 1929 the original vase was put up for sale at Christie's, but was withdrawn when it reached £29,000 (about $69,000). In 1946 the British Museum bought it.

Wedgwood died in 1795, and his son carried on the business, but he had not much heart for it. After the Battle of Waterloo (1815) the factory fell on hard times, and in 1828 the business was run down, although not completely closed. It was not revived until 1878.

Before going on to American porcelain, a word should be said about 'willow pattern'. This very

57
New England redware oval dish, inscribed 'Concord', of the late 18th century. American Museum in Britain, Claverton Manor, Bath.

58
Bennington parian porcelain figure of Red Riding Hood about 1855. Metropolitan Museum of Art, New York; gift of Dr Charles W. Green, 1947.

59
Examples of marks on porcelain.

Meissen
Crossed-sword mark adopted in
1723

Sèvres
Date-letter for 1753

Chelsea
Gold anchor *c.* 1756–1769

Crown Derby
1782–*c.* 1810

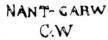
Nantgarw
1813–14; 1817–20

Worcester
1820

Rockingham
c. 1826–42

59

famous design for tableware and ornament came from China, probably via France, and was first used at the Caughley factory in 1780. Considerable variations in the pattern were introduced even in the early days of its use as a decoration. For example, the original design had 32 apples on the apple tree, the tallest tree by the pagoda on the right-hand side. Wedgwood gave the tree 34 apples; Rockingham excluded it altogether; Swansea varied the number of apples between 30 and 34; and Leeds gave the tree as many as 62 apples. There were many other variations, and the design was produced in many different colours.

American china is, regrettably, not a very rich field for collectors of 'antiques', using the strict meaning of the word. Little porcelain was made before 1850, and pottery was not really made on an industrial scale before about 1815.

Among the first experiments with porcelain-making in the 18th century were those undertaken by Andrew Duché, a Philadelphia-born potter who fabricated a good, crisp, translucent product, using kaolin. But he was discouraged from continuing, and only a very few pieces survive and these are mostly in museums. Other potters also tried, but not until the 19th century did anyone really succeed in making porcelain on a commercial basis. The pioneer was W. E. Tucker (1800–32), who was also a Philadelphian. Tucker showed his first pieces in 1826 and startled the discerning collectors of New England. A year later he began to win prizes for pieces exhibited at shows. His decorations included landscapes after Thomas Birch, imitation Sèvres styles, floral work, and heavy gilding. He made all kinds of tableware. It is expensive now, for he died in 1832 and not much has survived from the short period of his direction.

Another type of porcelain, called parian, was produced in America from about 1845. Parian, which was a biscuit porcelain (that is, an unglazed one), had been made by Spode's in Staffordshire, England, and it was used primarily for figures. It was intended to resemble marble, hence its name parian. C. W. Fenton, directing

potter of the Bennington pottery in Vermont, introduced his own brand, and it was a success. The Bennington factory made figures, but it also produced a variety of utilitarian ware, such as boxes, vases and jugs, in white, grey, blue and other shades, with relief decoration. Sometimes the jugs were glazed on the inside. This type of porcelain was of course imitated by other factories in America, but the Bennington pieces **58** probably remain the best.

Pottery in America hardly progressed beyond the manufacture of simple and useful items, such as pots and pans made by local potters for immediate use, until after the War of Independence. Much of it was made in red clay, and 'redware', as it is called, was widely used **57** for a long time. Sometimes it was decorated with brown yellow, black or green designs.

In the mid 18th century some emigrants from Staffordshire, who had been working in the potteries, started up in business in a small way, and they made simple and functional ware in red clay, with rich colour glazes. One type has become collectable now on both sides of the Atlantic, and this is New England redware. Another popular type was Pennsylvania-Dutch, which is quite different from the New England ware. Products included pie dishes, flower pots and tobacco jars, and some were decorated with *sgraffiato*. In this technique, the body of the item, after moulding, is covered with a white 'slip' (or white clay-and-water wash mix) and then glazed. The pattern is then cut into the slip surface to reveal the colour underneath. This type of ware continued until the mid 19th century.

Creamware, which was so successful in Britain, was introduced in America by the Bartlam pottery at Charleston in about 1770. It took a long time to acquire general popularity, like most other American pottery, and not until after the 1812–14 war did potteries make the sort of commercial impact that the Staffordshire and other factories had made in Britain in the middle of the 18th century. In the interval, Americans imported British and European ware in considerable quantities.

Glass

Glass is one field of antiques in which there are plenty of opportunities for collecting. To begin with, a great deal was made in the 18th and the early 19th centuries, not only in Britain but also in Europe and to a lesser extent in America. Many of the fine styles of the time were copied in the mid and late 19th century in great quantity, and although it is often possible to tell the copies from the originals, many of these imitations are fine pieces in themselves and so well worth collecting. In any case, by about 1980 they will begin to be regarded as antiques.

The variety of items made of glass was enormous, and it includes drinking glasses, jugs, sugar basins, salt cellars, scent bottles, sweet dishes, cream jugs, finger bowls, wine coolers, cake stands, fruit bowls, candlesticks, vases, ornaments and decanters. Rarer pieces include chandeliers, epergnes, plates, table lamps, witch balls, and yards-of-ale.

The most prolific use of glass, however, was for vessels associated with drinking, a habit enjoyed every bit as much then as it is today. You can generally find good examples of 18th- or early 19th-century glassware for drinking purposes in most salerooms or antique shops in town and country. Sets of six, eight or twelve glasses may be more difficult to find than twos or threes, and even when you do find them, you need to be careful that they are not made-up sets, that is, some genuine 18th-century and some good 19th-century imitations.

Drinking glasses are, in fact, the most popular pieces of glass to collect, and they have been for many years. A brief look at the background to these very attractive and functional pieces should help the collector to build up a good array, which, if chosen with care, will appreciate with time as well as make the dinner table complete.

The average 18th-century glass was made in two or three pieces, that is, bowl and stem in one piece joined to a foot, or bowl, stem and foot as separate entities, joined. The stem in a great many cases is the most important feature, for by its shape you can roughly, but only roughly, put a date to the glass. The shaped bulges in the stem are called knops, and these varied during the 18th century, the different styles overlapping.

The most sought-after glasses of this period are those with air-twist stems, although the baluster stems are **62** rarer, and also opaque twist stems. These are often, but mistakenly, thought to be Jacobean, but the air-twist stem did not emerge before about 1725, and the opaque twist, created by using enamel, either in white or in colour, did not come until about fifteen years later. A plain conical-shaped bowl on a white, opaque twist stem recently fetched £28 (about $67) in a country

60
Extremely rare posset pot of about 1676 by George Ravenscroft. It fetched £2,600 ($6,240) at Sotheby's, London, in 1967.

sale in Britain, but by now you may have to spend a little more.

A mid 18th-century variation of these most attractive twist stems is the incised twist, in which the stem is decorated externally by a number of closely rowed, twisted ribs, an idea which originated in Venice. Another variation is the mixed colour twist, produced roughly between 1760 and 1780. Meanwhile, the cut stem, which ran from 1740 for about seventy years, was often done in diamond or hexagonal-shaped facets. It was very popular, and it has been copied profusely from the middle of the 19th century onwards.

One feature of these 18th-century glasses is that they sparkle very brightly. Up to about 1675 English glass was heavy and dull in shading, but in 1674 George Ravenscroft discovered that if lead oxide was added in quantity to molten glass, the resulting glass was very fine and clear. Two years later he was making these new, clear glasses. The lead increased the density and so enhanced the power of the glass to disperse light. What is more, the glass bowl usually rang like a bell when struck. You will probably not find a Ravenscroft glass on the market, except perhaps at an important glass sale, but 17th-century glass of this kind is still obtainable in antique shops.

Glasses continued to be made heavy in style until 1745, when a Glass Excise Act was passed and a tax put on the materials used to make glass. Glasses thereafter became thinner and lighter. This tax was followed by later and similar ones having a serious effect on the industry, and the impositions were not lifted until 1845. From about the middle of the 18th century a glass manufacturing industry began to flourish in Ireland, chiefly because the Excise Act did not apply there. Thick glass was made and, as the style of cutting and engraving was popular, the finished glasses could be cut deeply with attractive patterns. In the early 19th century new styles of drinking glass appeared, and to-day these can still be found quite cheaply, though undamaged sets are obviously more expensive.

There are a number of ways of telling fakes from originals, but it really requires rather more than the application of one or more of the rules below, and in the long run the advice of an expert will be necessary. Up to about 1750, when a glass was blown, a jagged

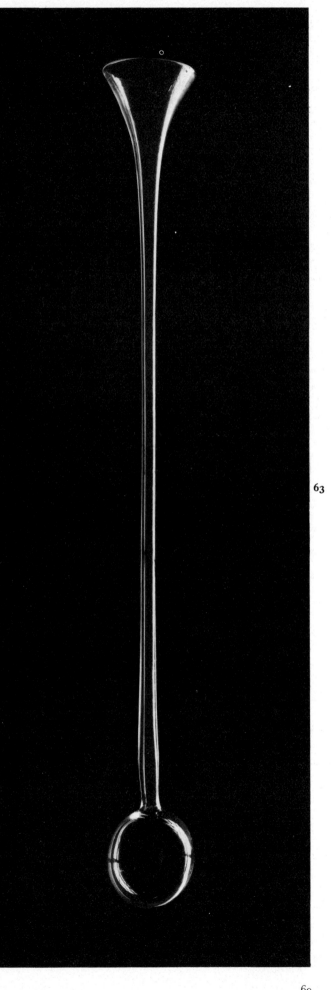

63

61
Early 19th-century English glasses, engraved with masonic insignia, in the manner of commemorative glass-engraving.

62
English glasses showing some of the various air-twist stems of the mid 18th century.

63
An 18th-century English 'yard-of-ale' glass. Victoria and Albert Museum, London.

surface was left on the base where the pipe was snapped off. This mark was called the 'pontil' mark. After 1750, glass-makers tended to grind the edges away to finish the product properly, and in the 19th century little trace of the pontil could be found in any glasses. These pontils can be faked, and faked well; look for scratches on the base, which suggest years and years of being drawn across surfaces. These scratches can also be faked, by using emery paper, but the scratch lines will be straight or circular, following the action of the abrasive used, whereas the scratches of time should be uneven.

The opaque twists of the mid 18th century can be imitated. The enamel used in the genuine article was dense white, with a touch of blue at the end of the twist. Copies made in the 19th century have a 'wishy-washy' look, and the spacing between the spirals is uneven. This is probably because to copy this pattern accurately takes more time than the job is worth.

One way to acquire judgment in these matters is to examine known fakes beside known genuine glasses, and the differences become apparent very quickly. But if you are not sure of your judgment, you can have a glass examined scientifically by special light rays or ultra-violet radiation. Glass made in the 18th century has a stress pattern very different from that of 19th- and 20th-century glass.

If you are going to collect drinking glasses, why not also build up a collection of bottles or decanters? These have been made in great quantity and variety over about 250 years. The earliest English bottles were made at the turn of the 17th century, and up to about 1720 they were generally of one shape—a globe with a flat bottom, short neck, and untidy lip. Little care was given to proportions. The colouring was greenish or brownish. After 1720 the globes thinned out to become cylindrical and the necks lengthened. Along with the bottle grew the decanter, which was generally much better designed and finished.

At first, the decanter was globular in shape and had a longish neck. The stopper had a ground edge to fit into the inside of the neck, also ground. Early stoppers were spire-shaped. By about the middle of the 18th century the globes had become the same shape as the bottle, that is, cylindrical. At this time it became customary

64

64

64
Two examples of Nailsea glass: (above) Gimmel flask with white enamel festooning, and (below) small jug with white enamel bands. Private Collection.

65
Engraved port decanter of about 1780.

66
A Bohemian clear glass tumbler with engraving cut through a ruby flash of about 1840. Victoria and Albert Museum, London.

to engrave and ornament with enamel the name of the liquor for which the decanter was to be used, such as PORT or CLARET, or a slogan like 'Truth and Loyalty'. One of the best-known decorators of glass at this time was William Beilby, of Newcastle-upon-Tyne, and pieces decorated by him are in great demand. The contents of a decanter were later indicated by the use of silver labels aptly engraved and suspended from small chains around the neck.

Two alternative types of decanter were developed later, both of which are still easy to find. These were the barrel-shaped type, variously decorated, and the square-shaped type, which generally have a ball-top stopper of cut glass in diamond-shaped facets. These square decanters were copied a great deal in the 19th century, and they appeared particularly in sets of three in a stand with a bar which prevented removal from the stand. These were called tantali, and although they are not yet classified as antiques, they soon will be.

Irish-made decanters are especially interesting to collectors, for they were very finely made. Four main factories produced quantities of good vessels: the Cork Glass Co., the Waterloo Co., and those at Waterford and Belfast. These decanters were usually of barrel shape, wider at the top than at the base, with three rings around the neck and with a mushroom stopper, cut in flutes. Although the basic design was similar, each factory had its own highly individual characteristics of engraved decoration. The high mark of Irish glass, however, was short-lived—from about 1770 to 1825—for in the latter year the Glass Excise Acts of England were extended to include Ireland.

Another, and not very common, clear piece of glass associated with drinking was the yard-of-ale. This was first designed in about 1690, and even had a foot like ordinary drinking glasses. Owing to its very fragile construction, not many have survived. In the 18th century they were made as a joke, and used in competitions at fairs and country gatherings. The idea was to fill them with beer and to see if you could drain the contents down without letting the last few tablespoonsful splash violently into your face. This is what usually happened because of the release of the air in the bulb, once the glass had been raised above the horizontal level for draining. Yards-of-ale were made again in Britain in the 19th century, now in a variety of colours, sometimes decorated, chiefly in the glass factories at Bristol and Nailsea.

Mention of Nailsea and Bristol brings us to coloured glass, a fascinating field for collecting. After the 1745 Glass Excise Act, a number of glass manufacturers in Bristol, who had for long been making window panes, bottles, and other household glass, turned to making light-weight articles in colour, as a substitute for earlier, heavier styles. Before long, other factories in Britain were also making coloured glass, not only at

65

66

67
Two Irish decanters: (left) one made by the Waterloo Co., and (right) another by the Cork Glass Co. Both are marked and were made in about 1820.

68
Three American glass decanters. (Left) early 19th-century blown, three-mould decanter of clear lead glass with a hollow ball stopper. (Centre) early 19th-century free-blown and engraved decanter of greenish-grey lead glass with a pressed stopper. (Right) late 18th-century free-blown, cut and engraved decanter of clear glass of the type made by the Amelung factory. American Museum in Britain, Claverton Manor, Bath; on loan from the Corning Museum of Glass, New York.

Nailsea in Somerset, but also in the Midlands, Yorkshire and Newcastle. The greatest quantities, however, were made at Bristol and Nailsea. One decorator of Bristol glass was Michael Edkins, whose designs have been preserved in the British Museum; another was I. Jacobs.

Real Bristol glass of the 18th century is hard to come by. The name Bristol has since come to cover almost any clear, blue glass of the period from English manufacturers, but it is really the name of a colour. So while you will not find much Bristol glassware of the 18th century, you can still collect blue clear glass. Articles included finger bowls, decanters, scent bottles, wineglass coolers, and cornucopias. A pair of genuine Bristol blue decanters fetched over £4,000 (about $8,600) in a sale in 1967, but a set of six blue finger bowls of the early 19th century, called 'Bristol' for the colour, fetched as little as £30 ($72).

From about 1790 coloured glass articles were made by the Nailsea manufacturers, and they specialised in curiosities like walking sticks, rolling pins, used by sailors sometimes for smuggling expensive scent, pocket flasks, jugs, vases and handbells.

Coloured glass was by no means the exclusive preserve of Britain. In ancient Roman times it had been made in the area of Venice, and it was just there that glass manufacture was reborn in the Middle Ages. From about AD 1000 bottles of various kinds were made. By the 1500s an industry had been established at Murano, and it was making clear glass, called *cristallo*. The products soon attracted the attention of Europe, and a vigorous export trade resulted. Venice was also making looking-glasses for the first time from silvered glass instead of highly polished metal.

Venetian glass was the finest in Europe for at least two centuries. In the 18th century, designers became bold and adventurous, and pieces reflected the taste for Rococo, so splendidly followed in furniture-making in Italy. Chandeliers of this period were often quite exquisite. The Murano factories declined in the Napoleonic era, but by about 1840 there was a great revival of glass manufacture, in which a multitude of earlier styles were reproduced. It is possible to collect these earlier 19th-century Venetian articles – bowls, cups, vases, epergnes, plates, candlesticks and so forth – at not too great a cost.

Another centre of glass manufacture that flourished for centuries was, and still is, Bohemia (approximately what is now Czechoslovakia and the south-eastern part of East Germany). In the Middle Ages, green, yellow and brown ornamental glass was made and marketed throughout Europe. In about 1670 the Bohemian craftsmen started to etch designs with hydrofluoric acid, a skill that is still practised today. Bohemian engraved glass was the finest in Europe for a long time, and English glass-makers often sent their wares to Breslau and other centres for etching. If you could find a piece of English glass etched in Bohemia you would indeed have a treasure, but to make a collection of these pieces would require a very substantial bank balance.

After about 1800 the Bohemian factories produced large quantities of coloured articles, and they made them very well. These are the sort of article you can collect, for although there are many of these pieces about they must appreciate in value. One style of interest can be found in the jet-black glass copies of English Wedgwood ware. Another speciality, later imitated elsewhere, was cased glass. Cased glass means the application of one layer of one colour on to another

73

69
Venetian *cristallo* wine glass with twisted baluster stem, of about 1600. Victoria and Albert Museum, London.

70
Late 17th-century American glass bottle from New England. American Museum in Britain, Claverton Manor, Bath.

71
Early 19th-century Venetian crystal chandelier with drops representing bunches of grapes with leaves.

69

70

Silver and Silver Plate

A silver article is not only attractive; as a rule it is also functional. Because the metal is precious any silver article has monetary value. Silver has two further advantages. It is almost indestructible, which means that there is still much old silver about for collecting. And, in Britain at any rate, it has for centuries had, by law, to be stamped to indicate that it has been assayed, or tested, by an assay office. This renders it much easier to date than, for example, a piece of copperware or a drinking glass.

These qualities immediately recommend silver objects for collecting. Whether they are also a means of investment is another matter, for this will to a great extent depend upon the condition of the silver and the skill with which it is fashioned. In the long term, even the poorer quality pieces must presumably appreciate in value, but this is not so over a short period. Between devaluation of the pound sterling in November 1967 and the end of 1968 antique silver prices rose by up to 300 per cent. Then, somewhat dramatically, they began to fall, and by June 1969 falls of nearly 50 per cent were registered. On the whole, the falls were found in the prices of the more conventional pieces, such as coffee pots and candlesticks, especially the poorer quality pieces. For example, a coffee pot made by Whipton in 1749 fetched £1,700 (about $4,080) at a sale in October 1968. In June 1969 a similar pot by Whipton, only slightly less well made, fetched only £700 (about $1,680). The same dealer bought both pots. In fact, quite a few people, hoping to make a quick profit, get their fingers burned. It is the sort of risk that a dealer must expect to run, but it is hard on the private collectors.

The value of silver cannot be related solely to its intrinsic price as a metal. Workmanship, age, style, quality, demand, all these need to be taken into account. When starting a collection of silver, therefore, there are two courses open to you. Either collect items because you like the look of them, and specialise, for instance, in silver snuff boxes (late George IV ones can still be obtained cheaply) or in silver figures. Or, accumulate silver which has more definite appreciative value. For this, however, you will need to study silver closely; you must get to know what well-informed dealers and collectors are looking for, and concentrate on a few good pieces that really do have quality. Because of the large amount available, whether good, medium or poor quality, you should be able to follow either course. Money will be the limiting factor.

Silver has been made in a great many countries, and we can only look at the silver which you are most likely to encounter in Britain or the United States. All four nations of the British Isles have produced silver and, on

74
Italian 16th-century knife, fork and spoon assembly by Antonio Gentili. Metropolitan Museum of Art, New York; Rogers Fund.

75
Selection of English silver spoons of the late 17th and early
18th centuries. (Left to right) spoon of rat-tail pattern with flat
handle and lobed end by Thomas Spackman bearing the London
hall-mark for 1709–10; spoon of rat-tail pattern with the
London hall-mark for 1715–16; late 17th-century spoon bearing
the Taunton hall-mark, with elliptical bowl decorated with
relief scroll-work and with flat handle lobed and turned at the
end; front of a spoon of similar pattern to that second from the
left; spoon by Thomas Jackson bearing the London hall-mark
for 1743–4, with ridged handle turned at the end.

76
Silver coffee pot, with the London hall-mark, dated 1706.
Victoria and Albert Museum, London.

77
Unusual pair of George III table candlesticks, made by the
Hester Bateman business in 1781. These fetched £2,500 (about
$6,000) at Christie's, London, in October 1969.

the whole, it has been of the best quality in the world.
American silver is fine, but it is not generally marked,
which is in itself an interesting collecting point. Italian
silver is possibly the best example of European silver.

Let us take a look at the official stamping of silver
in Britain. There are five possible marks to be found on
properly assayed silver. The hall-mark is strictly
speaking the mark which establishes the hall, or assay
office, of the town where the piece was assayed.
London's mark is a leopard's head and was first used in
the reign of Edward IV (1461–83). It has continued in
use up to the present day, except for a period of 22
years, from 1697 to 1719, to which we shall return later.
Assay offices were set up in various towns in Britain,
some of which are no longer operating. The assay
offices were (or are): Birmingham, since 1773, mark:
an anchor; Chester, from 1686 to 1962, mark: three
wheatsheaves and sword; Dublin, since 1638, mark: a
harp; Edinburgh, since 1681, mark: a castle, and other
marks; Exeter, from 1701 to 1883, various marks
including a castle; Glasgow, from 1819 to 1964, mark:
a tree with bird in branches, or variations; Newcastle,
from 1701 to 1884, mark: three castles; Sheffield, since
1773, mark: a crown; Norwich, from 1565 to 1701,
mark: a castle and lion; York, from 1560 to 1858,
various marks.

The term hall-mark has now come to embrace the whole set of marks found on silver, and this includes the maker's mark, the date letter and the standard mark. The sovereign's head duty mark was also used from 1784 to 1890.

Until about 1840 the maker's mark was generally, though not always, the initials of the maker. The date letter establishes the year of assay, and it is a single letter in a certain print style inside a shield of one shape or another. Together with the town assay mark, identification of a piece of silver can now be made, in principle. The lettering, however, requires much more careful studying than may at first be supposed. The order of date letters varies. Because the letters are so small it is possible to confuse one in one cycle with another in a later, or earlier, cycle. For example, a capital Roman O, which is the London letter for 1809, is very like the small O for 1829. The difference in this case is checked by reference to the town mark. In the former year the leopard's head had a crown on it, and in 1829 it did not.

The standard mark is meant to show that the article is of the correct quality, that is, the sterling standard, established in 1300 and maintained until 1697, and then restored in 1720. The sterling standard is 925 parts of silver in 1,000, which is higher than continental European silver. The standard mark is a lion passant for England. In 1697 the Government introduced a new and higher silver standard, to counteract the tendency among silversmiths to melt down coins and use them to make their pieces. This new standard was called Britannia, the mark being a figure of Britannia. It replaced the lion until 1720. When the old sterling standard was restored in 1720, the lion was also restored, but the Britannia mark was retained for those pieces which continued to be made of the Britannia standard. It is still used on those pieces, which nowadays are almost limited to presentation articles.

The fifth mark was the sovereign's head, which was stamped on silver from 1784 to 1890. It was used to record that the duty required had been paid. The duty was not paid on very small pieces.

You will see at once that there is an opportunity here for forgery, and our Victorian grandfathers went in for this on a large scale. Earlier generations also tampered with marks, but often for different reasons. False marks are imitations of old marks. They have been perpetrated by forgers for the express purpose of deceiving, and thereby accumulating more money. Detecting these false marks is very difficult, and it is only possible after years of experience of handling antique silver. A false mark may look too new for the alleged age of the piece,

76   77

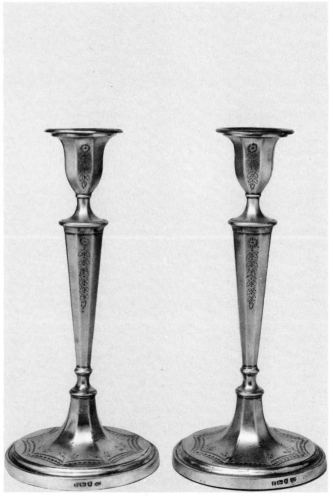

79   78

78
Travelling table service made towards the end of the 18th century by the Italian silversmith Valadini for Cardinal York. Royal Library, Windsor Castle.

79
A very clear set of marks on the base of a dinner plate made by Paul Storr, the famous Regency silversmith. (Left to right) Storr's mark; the sterling standard mark; the crowned leopard's head representing the London mark; the date letter, 1810; the duty mark, the sovereign's head (George III). Worshipful Company of Goldsmiths, London.

80
Fine example of Scottish silver by Robertson of Edinburgh. This is a bannock rack, dated 1773. Royal Scottish Museum, Edinburgh.

81
George IV silver snuff box, made in Birmingham in 1829.

that is, it may not reveal enough wear round the edges where it was stamped into the metal. But even this could be overcome by the simple expedient of claiming that, for example, the faked set of spoons was made for Lord X in 1765 but that he died before using them and they have remained wrapped up in soft cloth in the family bureau ever since. This sort of claim was believed in Victorian days, but it would be unlikely to be accepted today unless substantial proof were forthcoming.

An easier type of forgery to detect is the piece made, for example, in 1890, alleged to be 1750 and given the required marks, but which does not really fit into the styles of 1750. There are not many of these about and here is a field for the collector.

Another type of mark tampering was transposition. Transposed marks are marks lifted bodily out of a piece and moulded into another piece. If done in the early days of silver-making it would often be because the silversmith did not wish to incur the expense of having a piece assayed. It was, of course, illegal. Our Victorian forgers soon learned this procedure and adapted it to pure misrepresentation on their bogus pieces. Many are very difficult to detect.

The variety of articles made in silver is extensive. It includes knives, forks, spoons, sauceboats, salt cellars, pepper pots, sugar casters, entrée dishes, cream jugs, candlesticks, wine coasters, salvers, tea and coffee pots, cups, porringers, toast racks, dishes, plates, tureens, snuff boxes, card cases, ornaments, tankards and many other items. Of all these, spoons have perhaps survived in greater quantities and variety. They are probably the most widely used utensils in both dining rooms and kitchens, and more than thirty different types were at

80

81

one time or another in constant usage in nearly every household.

The apostle spoon is so named because the handle part is a figure of Christ or of one of the disciples. They were popular from Renaissance times until about 1685 (the death of Charles II), but they have also been copied. Caddy spoons are in considerable demand these days. They are not only very attractive in the variety of design but they are also useful. They are short-handled, and were designed in shapes such as leaves, birds, and so on. One much sought-after style is the jockey-cap motif. Prices depend to a great extent on the quality of design and execution, but an attractive one, about 150 years old, can be obtained cheaply.

Marrow spoons are long and straight, with narrow bowls. Used to scoop out marrow from bones, each end has a bowl of different size. Straining spoons are worth collecting, too. The bowl part is pierced, sometimes with a fine pattern.

Tea spoons, probably the most prolific of all spoons, were sometimes small versions of table or dessert spoons. They did not come in sets much before the 18th century, but the designs have, on the whole, been more adventurous. Stems might be foliage-shaped or carved or spiralled, and even the bowls were unconventional. So many tea spoons have been made that it would be quite easy to start collecting them. An interesting beginning could be made by visiting some of the antique markets such as the stalls and booths in Portobello Road, London. By the end of the day you could probably have a dozen different, single spoons for a very small outlay, but it would be as well to take a book of silver marks with you as quite a number of traders do not trouble to look them up. The spoons are sold for a price based on what the traders paid for them. A useful, cheap, pocket-sized book of marks is *British and Irish Silver Assay Office Marks, 1544–1968*, by F. Bradbury.

Silver-making has had its share of fine craftsmen. Among the best known in British silver history were Paul de Lamerie, Paul Storr, the Courtauld family, and the Scotsman, Robertson. Hester Bateman is also a 80 famous name in the world of silver, but it is doubtful 77 whether she herself made much of the silver attributed to her, and whether the name does not, in fact, cover articles produced in her workshop, which she continued to operate after the early death of her husband.

Lamerie was a Huguenot from what is now Belgium. He settled in London in Queen Anne's reign and first registered pieces in 1711. Lamerie worked in both sterling and Britannia silver. His artistry is exceptionally fine, and his interpretation of the Rococo is unequalled. Lamerie pieces now fetch enormous prices. Hester Bateman silver, very popular with American

83

84

84

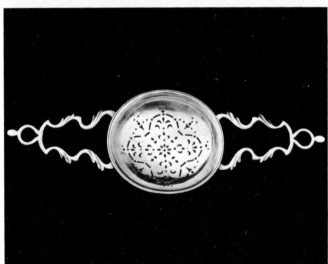

85

86

82
English salver of Sheffield plate of about 1820. Victoria and Albert Museum, London.

83
George III entrée dish and lid, dated 1788.

84
American silver tea and coffee service made in 1828 by Samuel Kirk of Baltimore. Brooklyn Museum, New York; gift of Mr and Mrs Richman Proskauer.

85
Interesting piece of American silver made before the War of Independence: a punch strainer made by Samuel Minott of Boston in about 1765. American Museum in Britain, Claverton Manor, Bath.

86
Three American silver porringers. (Left) early 18th-century porringer by William James of Marblehead, Massachusetts. (Above right) late 18th-century porringer by Bancroft Woodcock of Wilmington, Delaware. (Below right) porringer made in 1738 by John Brevoort of New York. American Museum in Britain, Claverton Manor, Bath; the two items on the right on loan from the Metropolitan Museum of Art, New York.

collectors, is of high quality but not in the same class as Lamerie's work. Storr, on the other hand, became in

79 his time the best known silversmith in England. He worked in London in the first twenty or so years of the 19th century, approximately the period of the Regency. He made considerable quantities of the finest silver for the Prince of Wales.

When collecting silver, you should not overlook Sheffield plate. It was invented in about 1743 by Thomas Bolsover in Sheffield. He fused a thin layer of silver on to a thicker layer of copper, rolled it out in such a way that the metals remained more or less in the same proportion, and then fashioned the pieces. It was a fine substitute for real silver and by the 1760s had become a rival in production. All manner of articles were made of it, and they were, of course, much cheaper. Homes which hitherto had had to make do without silver, or anything like it, now could have this good quality plate on the table. To begin with, the plate was marked by the initials of the maker. Then, for a while, trade marks were introduced. Sheffield plate fell from demand when the process of electroplating base metal with a very thin coating of silver came into being in 1840.

82 Sheffield plate articles to look for include candlesticks (silver ones are not common and are expensive), muffineers, wine coasters (generally with green baize bases), candle snuffers, salvers, ladles and knife rests.

6 American silver in its earlier years closely followed British styles, and it was made by craftsmen who had served their apprenticeship in London or elsewhere and emigrated to the New World. It seems that few items of these early years have survived, possibly because much silver had to be melted down during the War of Independence to provide ready money. (In the Civil War in England, 1642–7, both Royalists and Parliamentarians were driven to similar extremes.) Consequently,

86 even the simplest pieces, such as spoons or porringers, are very hard to come by and on either side of the Atlantic are expensive.

After the war, Americans began to make their own silver in considerable quantities. They copied British styles, but they adapted European styles as well. American silver was not generally marked as fully as the British pieces, despite the fact that the standard was usually as high. Makers usually stamped their initials.

The easiest pieces to acquire are commemorative spoons, some of which have most original handles, such as crocodiles, Red Indians, or even spades. Other pieces for collecting are sugar tongs, which lend themselves to all manner of extremes in design, decanter labels, soap

85 tins and punch strainers.

Several American silversmiths were as skilled as the best British craftsmen, and even as early as the 1630s Robert Sanderson, who emigrated to Boston and set up in business, was making pieces of the highest quality of workmanship. Perhaps the most famous, however, was

Paul Revere (1735–1818), who specialised in Rococo and Classical styles and has been called the American de Lamerie.

Revere has a particularly romantic aura about him. He was the son of a Huguenot emigrant, Apollos Rivoire, who was apprenticed as a goldsmith in Boston. Paul, whose father altered his name to Revere, was similarly apprenticed as a young man. He also learned the art of engraving. As a young man he became caught up in the Independence movement, and was actually involved in the affair of the Boston Tea Party in 1773. In 1775 Revere rode through the night from Boston to Lexington to warn the Colonists that the British army was on the march against them. This ride was later immortalised by Longfellow's poem *The Midnight Ride of Paul Revere.*

When he was not harassing the British, Revere designed the first official seal of the Colonists, and he also designed and printed money. He found time, too, to investigate the properties of copper and introduced the process of rolling it. On top of all this, Revere also made some very fine silver, usually marked with his surname in a rectangle. Experienced and wealthy collectors are fond of Revere silver, but in general it would be too expensive for the average buyer.

Early in the 19th century, in Baltimore, silver was made which was marked not only with manufacturers' initials or trade marks but also with date letters. This practice continued for about sixteen years (1814–30). Baltimore silver of this period could be a good field for collection.

Returning to Europe briefly, Italian silver is a favourite with collectors, but it is, in general, expensive. In its earliest forms it is truly representative of the high genius of the Renaissance. In the 16th century such craftsmen as Benvenuto Cellini (1500–69), the sculptor, and Antonio Gentili (c. 1520–1609) were making articles with exquisite skill. Over the next 200 years or more, there followed a procession of superb silversmiths, who made quantities of extremely beautiful silver. Nineteenth-century copies of the earlier styles are circulating among dealers and occasionally appear in sale catalogues. Even if the piece looks untidy or suspect, it may be worth buying, in the same way that 19th-century Venetian glass is now highly collectable. Before very long some of it will be accepted as antique.

87
A fine collection of old English silver. (Top, left to right) one of a pair of George II sugar dredgers made by Samuel Wood in 1743; one of a pair of George III waiters with bead borders made by Robert Jones and John Schofield in 1776. (Second row, left to right) small Charles II tankard with chinoiserie decoration made in 1683; early Victorian beaded and engraved tea pot with ivory handle; George III chamber candlestick with snuffer, dated 1815. (Third row, left to right) one of a set of George III salt cellars of 1790; George III sweetmeat dish of about 1765. (Bottom) George IV meat skewer of 1825.

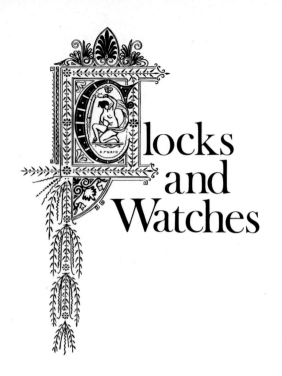

Clocks and Watches

Collecting clocks is a fascinating but somewhat anti-social pastime. Clocks are so varied in size, shape, type of face, mechanism and sound of striking, that even a small collection would attract immediate attention. This would be enhanced if all the clocks struck the hours and half-hours at more or less the right time, but the question arises, how long could one bear all that irregular tick-ticking and striking in one room anywhere in the house? Where, indeed, would one put a collection of clocks? The beginner could put one in each room, then two, and possibly go as far as three, but after that the noise problem is bound to arise. Still, these problems should not deter one from collecting clocks, which are, in the great majority of cases, extremely fine works of art to have about the house.

Mechanical clocks have been made for centuries, since the 1400s at least, but survivors more than 250 years old are not at all common, and whenever they do come on the market are extremely expensive to buy.

If you intend to buy clocks, always check that they are working properly, for repairs are costly today and the people who understand these old pieces become rarer every decade. Despite the enormous variety of faces, case shapes, and sizes, clocks since about 1600 fit nicely into six main categories: lantern clocks, bracket and mantel clocks, longcase clocks, carriage clocks, wall clocks, and other decorative clocks.

Lantern clocks are probably of English origin. A few were made in the Elizabethan era, but they were popular throughout the 17th century and persisted in some provincial areas into the 18th century. They look like ship's lanterns, and they used to hang on walls from a bracket in much the same way. They were made of silver or brass or other metal, and they had a bell at the top for striking. These clocks were not particularly accurate, and could lose or gain as much as twenty minutes a day. Their accuracy used to be checked by using a sundial. Lantern clocks were driven by weights regulated by a balance beneath the dome bell at the top. They would be difficult to forge now, but imitations of the type are made in quantity. Some of the original clocks were converted and given a pendulum movement after the introduction of the pendulum in the 1650s.

The isochronous properties of the pendulum were discovered in 1582 by the Italian mathematician and astronomer, Galileo Galilei. He further understood that, if applied to clocks, the pendulum would make them far more accurate than they currently were. With his son he experimented with a timepiece, but for some reason unknown did not pursue the matter, and it was

88
Miniature bracket clock with basket top, by Thomas Tompion. Made in about 1700, it is typical of the bracket clocks of this distinguished craftsman.

89
Very fine American ba[...]
American Museum in [...]

90
French clock of about [...]
ebony, with a wheel ba[...]
Wallace Collection, Lo[...]

94   **95**

not until 1656 that the Dutch mathematician and physicist, Christiaan Huygens (1629–95), used a pendulum to regulate a clock accurately over a period of time. Two years later, John Fromanteel, an English clockmaker, brought the principle to England.

The first pendulum clocks were short, and the pendulums swung quickly over a wide arc. Many of the clocks were conversions of the balance-regulated lantern ones. But soon it was realised that a longer pendulum would provide greater accuracy–and require less space in which to swing–and so arose the longcase clock.

93
Fine lantern clock of 1676 in silver case, signed by Edward Webbe. Victoria and Albert Museum, London.

94
Early carriage clock of the 19th century, made in England by Dent. This firm also made the clock for Big Ben at the Houses of Parliament in London.

95
Unusual clock, made in the shape of a miniature secretaire, with turquoise-blue plaques of Sèvres porcelain. It was made in the late 18th century by Cronier of Paris. Wallace Collection, London.

The longcase clock originated in England and became famous throughout the world. The earliest ones were made in oak cases, veneered or decorated with ebony, but when walnut moved into the foremost position for furniture-making, in the late 17th and early 18th centuries, longcase clocks were built in walnut, usually in the figured or oyster veneer pattern, occasionally with marquetry in most beautiful colour and design, and also in lacquer. Many longcase clocks were made, some by the foremost craftsmen of the age, including Thomas Tompion, Joseph Knibb, John **92** Fromanteel, Samuel Stokes, and William Webster, and if such clocks can be shown to have come from such workshops, they are extremely valuable. A Knibb longcase clock fetched £9,000 (about $21,600) in 1968. After the mid 18th century, when clock cases were made in mahogany and in considerable numbers, the quality is often lower, and the value today is much less. British provincial craftsmen continued to make the cases in oak and walnut, and carried on into the 19th century. An oak clock with a brass face fetched £25 (about $60) at a sale in Norfolk in 1968.

These longcase clocks are generally either over 6 feet 6 inches high–even as much as 7 feet 6 inches–or under 6 feet. The former are called 'grandfather' clocks, a term that came into use early in the 19th century, and

the latter type 'grandmother' clocks. Grandfathers of the 19th century are not really very valuable unless made by a good craftsman. An Act of Parliament of 1698 stipulated that all clock-makers should inscribe their names and the town of manufacture somewhere on the clock, and often, though not always, this is found on the face.

A word should be said about the dials and the hoods. Dials of the 17th century were as a rule 10 inches or less in diameter, but after about 1700 you will find the dimension has increased to 12 or more inches. The larger face is typical of later clocks, but it does not rule out dials of 10 inches made in the provinces as late as 1800. At first the dials were silver or brass or some other metal but in the 18th century clock-makers began to paint dials on metal or even wooden backgrounds. They also added refinements such as mechanisms to record the phases of the moon or days of the month, second-hands, and so forth. Dating was done, of course, on 17th-century clocks, and very intricately, too, notably by Tompion, who introduced the perpetual calendar on some of his clocks.

The hoods of longcase clocks followed the architectural styles of the day, and Queen Anne and early Georgian examples had typical Baroque ornament, broken pediments, scrollwork, flanked by pillars which were spiralled or turned. Mid 18th-century clock hoods were more restrained and Classical. Late 18th- and early 19th-century imitations were of all styles; the Baroque mixed with the Classical, for example.

Another kind of clock introduced in the 17th century was the bracket clock. To begin with this meant a portable clock which stood on a table or on a special wall bracket. They were sometimes wound by pulling strings. The early ones were driven by a spring mechanism. Their cases, also, had architectural features with a great variety of ornament. Some very fine pieces were made, but by the end of the 18th century these clocks were becoming quite common, for by then an enormous number of houses had mantelpieces on which to put them. For this reason they are sometimes called mantel clocks.

If you are going to collect clocks seriously, one or two other types will come your way. One is wrongly called the Act of Parliament clock. This time-piece is driven by hanging weights. It has a large dial, generally unglazed. The clocks are supposed to have been introduced in the late 18th century, so that inn-keepers could provide the time for customers who refused to buy clocks or watches because of a tax put on them by William Pitt the Younger, prime minister from 1783 to 1801. In fact, although there are some of these clocks in public houses around Britain (there is one at the Rose & Crown, West Lyng, near Taunton) they were undoubtedly made much earlier than this. They are not always very attractive, nor are they often very well made. One fetched £10 (about $24) at a sale in 1967. Evidently the local publican did not wish to have it as additional décor to his house.

There is one type of clock you will see in shops throughout Britain. This is the carriage clock, used for the long distances covered in the 19th century by coach and rail. It is usually rectangular in shape, with thick glass walls and shiny brass or ormulu vertical frame, top and base. The front is usually of white enamel behind the glass, and the face may have more than one dial, for instance, one for the time, one for the day of the month, and one for the month. The clock should have a leather-covered case, with a sliding panel in one face which can be removed to reveal the face. Another feature is a button on the lid which, when pressed, connects with the button on top of the clock, and this activates a mechanism enabling the clock to strike the nearest hour. But despite the glamorous and superficially luxurious appearance of the carriage clock, it will almost certainly not be more than 120 years old, possibly much less, for it is a 19th-century innovation. The best had French movements inside an English-made case. Astonishingly, these carriage clocks fetch very high prices.

The other time-piece we have not yet mentioned is the watch. Although nearly everyone has one these days, few people perhaps realise that craftsmen were making watches nearly 500 years ago. In those days, and for about two and a half centuries, they were somewhat larger, spherical or drum-shaped, or soap-tin-shaped, and they were more like portable clocks. They did not keep good time, for the mechanism was at first a mainspring operating through a succession of wheels. But the casings were invariably most beautifully made and decorated.

In 1675 Huygens, who had revolutionised clock-making twenty years earlier, introduced a method of controlling the movement of a watch so that it kept good time. This was the spiral balance spring. A French watch-maker fashioned the first one, and after that watch-making entered into the lists as an important industry in Europe. The best watches for a while came from England, but in the 18th century French watches presented a serious challenge. As the years went by watch-makers strove to achieve greater accuracy of manufacture and time-keeping, and they also tried to get all the parts into a smaller casing, so that watches became less bulky. But nothing was spared in the

96

Selection of antique watches: (top left) French flat gold and enamel watch of about 1810; (centre right) flat gold and enamel scalloped watch made in Geneva in about 1820; (centre) English gold and enamel watch of 1835, with matching fob; (bottom left) watch of gold, enamel, garnets and zircons made in Paris in about 1775; (bottom right) French or Swiss gold watch of about 1795, with transparent enamel laid on an engine-turned ground.

97

97
American tall clock of about 1770, with mahogany case.
Museum of Fine Arts, Boston; M. & M. Karolik Collection.

98
American shelf clock made by Smith and Goodrich.

99
Unusual watch with a windmill sail for the second-hand. It was
made in London. The silver case is dated 1802.

100
Octagonal watch in a silver case made in about 1630. The back
cover is engraved with the figures of Pluto and Proserpine.

99

100

decoration. Dials were enamelled or silvered; they were given Roman or Arabic numerals and were fitted with fine blue steel hands; and different small dials were incorporated for seconds, dates and seasons. The cases were similarly treated in a variety of materials including tortoiseshell, gold, enamel, gold inlay on leather, porcelain and silver. As early as 1705 Fromanteel made a watch with an alarm arrangement.

A popular watch for collecting is the 'hunter'. This has a cover for the front glass and another for the rear part of the watch. The 'half-hunter' is a watch which has a small circle of glass in the centre of the front cover, through which you can see the position of the hands. These hunters and half-hunters are quite common, although an almost infinite variety of decoration exists which alone makes hunters worth collecting. Some were made by the great clock-makers, such as Tompion, Ellicott and Massey, but these are extremely expensive. Dealers often buy hunters for the metal value, and possibly the spare parts.

American clocks provide a splendid field for the collector. For the first years they are little more than copies of English clocks. The Colonists were very fond of longcase clocks, of both sizes, and after the War of Independence they began to make them in great quantities. The hoods reflected the furniture styles of the time, just as in England. The cases were made of mahogany, pinewood, or cherrywood, and a great deal of skill and care was put into the case. Some craftsmen, wishing to economise, made the moving parts in wood, and they made them so well that little loss of accuracy

in time-keeping was experienced. Such pieces were made by Cheney of Hartford, Massachusetts, Gideon Roberts, and others, and are now sought eagerly by collectors.

American clock-makers also devoted their talents to making wall clocks of one kind or another. They introduced two most original and attractive types, the 'banjo' and the 'shelf'. The banjo was first produced **89** by the clock-making business of the Willard family in Massachusetts at the turn of the 19th century. These clocks had eight-day movements and they kept extremely good time. Willard banjo clocks are now sought on both sides of the Atlantic. Many visiting American service personnel, stationed in Britain for two- or three-year periods of service, have sold these enchanting clocks to local salerooms or shops, and replaced them with British carriage clocks or some other decorated variety.

The shelf clock is an amusing piece, although not of **98** very high craftsmanship. When they were first made, 150 years ago, they were intended for export to Britain, where they can still be found. One of the leading makers of these quaint pieces was Eli Terry, and many of his shelf clocks were made of wooden parts, because brass was expensive. The casing was of course the point of interest. It stood about 2 feet (610 mm.) high. In principle it was an architectural front, with pillar sides, broken arch top, or Gothic top, or even swan's neck pediment. Below the dial was a painting or decorated panel of some kind. After about 1840 brass working parts were re-introduced and completely superseded the wooden ones.

Old Prints

Prints are a splendid field for the collector. They are superbly decorative and can often be obtained quite cheaply. If you ever longed to fill your house with pictures but thought you would never have the money to do so, then start collecting prints. At present many prints are underpriced–good ones can from time to time be found for between £1 and £2 in Britain, or a few dollars in the United States–and this is largely because print-making is not properly accorded the respect it deserves as an art. A print is not merely a reproduction: it is a work of art. There is an enormous range of subjects on which prints have been made, and even the frames in which they are obtainable often have a variety of their own.

A print is an impression taken from a block or plate which has on it a picture produced by one or other of a number of processes, by hand or by machine. This impression, furthermore, can be multiplied, within limits, and with no decline in the quality of reproduction. Prints can be produced in several colours, in black and white, or in other two-tone combinations. Among the best loved colour prints are sporting prints, especially those associated with hunting, a pastime enjoyed more widely 150 years ago than it is today. H. T. Alken (1785–1851) engraved a vast number of these depicting every aspect of this sport, and other sports, too, like racing and fishing. Many of his own designs were copied by later engravers.

The principal processes used were line-engraving, etching, mezzotinting, aquatinting, stipple-engraving, and lithography. A line-engraving is one cut directly in lines with a special tool on a copper or zinc plate. The plate is inked and put into a press, and copies are then run off. Variation in tone is achieved by engraving the lines closely or not so closely, as required. This was the major process used in the 17th and 18th centuries. If colouring was required, the plate was inked with different coloured inks in the correct places, or several plates of one picture were engraved and one plate was used for each colour in the right place. The results were not always very good, and many print-makers preferred to colour the black and white outline print by hand afterwards.

Two celebrated engravers of the 18th century were William Hogarth (1697–1764) and George Vertue (1684–1756). Vertue specialised in portraiture, and engraved or etched pictures of nearly every famous person of his century, together with many notables of earlier days. He produced a series of pictures of the kings of England, taken generally from authentic sources like stained-glass windows, recumbent statues,

101

Two bunches a penny, primroses, two bunches a penny. One of a series of *The Cries of London*, stipple-engraved by L. Schiavonetti from paintings by F. Wheatley and published by Colnaghi.

98

Veduta di Campo Vaccino

102
View of Campo Vaccino, an etching by Giovanni Battista Piranesi (1720-78).

103
A Modern Belle going to the Rooms at Bath, an etching by James Gillray, (1757-1815), the famous caricaturist. Victoria and Albert Museum, London.

104
Engraving of Charles II by George Vertue, dated about 1736.

A Modern Belle going to the Rooms at Bath.

DIEU ET MON DROIT

CHARLES II.
KING of ENGLAND, SCOTLAND, FRANCE & IRELAND,
Defender of the Faith &c.

105
Check, etched by H. Alken of London in 1823.

106
*Capture of the British Frigate Gurriere by the U.S. Frigate
Constitution*, engraved by D. Kimberley, after Thomas Birch.
John Judkyn Memorial, Freshford, Bath.

or oil paintings. These 'king' prints can still be found
quite cheaply, though they are not likely to be first
111 editions. Hogarth, who was also a celebrated painter,
demonstrated that engraving could be profitable as well
as aesthetic, and he became rich through his series on
the evils of London. *The Rake's Progress* and *The
Harlot's Progress* are just two of the series which enjoyed
immense popularity. They are also fine social docu-
ments, for they reveal, probably better than any verbal
description, some of the worst aspects of London life in
the 18th century. Prints of *The Harlot's Progress* are said
to have sold over 1,000 copies in the first edition.

103 The etching process, favoured by many French and
Italian artists as well as English ones, was as follows. A
copper plate was waxed over, and the required design
cut in the wax with a fine needle. The design was then
enabled to 'bite' into the plate by immersing it in a
solution of hydrochloric or nitric acid. The inks were
applied to fill up the 'bitten' lines and shapes, and the
plate was then pressed on to the paper. The tone was
determined by the length of time the plate was left in

the acid bath. Etching was introduced into England
by the Bohemian artist Wenceslaus Hollar (1607–77), **11**
who in his time produced over 2,000 different etchings,
covering a wide field of topics, religious, urban, rural
and portraits.

Another process, championed in England by Prince
Rupert of the Rhine, the nephew of Charles I, was
mezzotinting. This is engraving which emphasises
features by darkness of tone. These dark tones are obtained by making the plate rough all over and then
smoothing those parts which are to appear in lighter
shade. The lines of line-engraving all but disappear, and
the effect produced is not unlike that of an oil painting.
Akin to mezzotinting was aquatinting. Here, the plate **10**
was covered with a resin, the resin worked on, and acid
applied and left to work its way on to the surface of the
plate. A colour print by this process looks something
like a water colour, which in many cases it was intended
to do.

The technique of stipple-engraving entailed the use
of a needle point on the plate to produce hundreds of
dots and dashes in order to create tone effect. The
resulting prints were often of extremely high quality.
Among the best-known artists who used the stipple
method were William Ward (1762–1826) and Fran-
cesco Bartolozzi (1728–1815). Bartolozzi was Floren-
tine. He moved to England in 1764 and was soon
appointed engraver to George III. He was also one of

the original members of the Royal Academy. His engravings covered reproductions of works by many painters, including Giordano, Reynolds, Cipriani and Gainsborough. He also produced copies of well-known Tudor portraits by Holbein and others. But perhaps the best-known of his range were the Classical pieces, and the allusions to ideals. A great many Bartolozzi prints were run off, and it would not be difficult to build up a collection, although you would have to pay quite dearly for the earliest editions.

One very famous set of stipple-engravings which sold extremely well at the end of the 18th century was *The Cries of London* series. These were thirteen prints stipple-engraved after original paintings by Francis Wheatley. The engraving was done by Schiavonetti and Cardon, and published by Colnaghi, a firm still in business in London. Imitations soon appeared, and unless you are experienced, you will find it difficult to distinguish between originals and copies, and in attempting to build up a set, you may end up with a mixture of the two. A reputable dealer, however, should put you right.

Thomas Bewick (1753–1828) was an artist who re-introduced the art of engraving on wood, specialising in natural subjects such as birds and plants. He used boxwood and cut the drawings against the grain for effect. Wood blocks were still being used by some illustrators for newspapers as late as 1914.

The last major printing process to mention here is lithography. This was introduced at the end of the 18th century. It is basically a chemical process. The picture is drawn on a flat, smooth piece of stone with a special pencil containing grease. A film of water is spread across the stone. The drawn parts will reject the water. When the ink, which is greasy, is rolled on to the stone, only the drawing will accept it, and thus an impression can be made. Lithography has been an extremely popular form of print-making. Copies of lithographs can be multiplied in considerable numbers without decline in quality of reproduction. Sometimes the effect is almost photographic.

It is not easy to draw up rules for recognising good prints, except that sharp definition generally suggests an early edition. Various efforts were made by well-known artists to protect themselves from plagiarism, but they were not always successful. On the whole, the high degree of skill displayed by, for example, Hogarth, or Alken, or Bartolozzi, or Hollar, would be recognisable after one had spent some time studying their original work against their imitators. But since so many attractive prints, well coloured and with a fair degree of definition, can often be obtained cheaply, perhaps their origins are not so important.

If you want to collect prints for their subject-matter and not for the artist or the school of art, it is still possible to buy an old book which contains many prints illustrating the theme of the work. Sometimes these books were produced more to demonstrate the skill and beauty of the prints than to publicise the writing. These prints can be detached from the book, and though this may seem like vandalism, it is done on a wide scale. A great many prints found loose now in portfolios in print shops began as illustrations bound in a volume. I once knew a man who found two green leather volumes, of about 1810, containing prints of about 200 worthies of the 18th century, with thumbnail sketches of their life stories. The prints were copies of Vertue portraits. He removed all the prints and papered the walls of a small room with them, tidily in rows. It was certainly an unusual form of decoration.

You can extend your horizons in print collecting by picking up a few 18th-century prints from the continent

107
An 18th-century print of Watteau's painting *Amusements Champêtres*. British Museum, London.

108
Sir Joshua Reynolds's painting *Jane Countess of Harrington, Lord Viscount Petersham, and the Hon. Lincoln Stanhope*, engraved by F. Bartolozzi (1728-1815).

of Europe, where the art of print-making was no less popular or skilled. In France, Antoine Watteau (1684–1721) produced some extremely fine etchings, and some of these were copied by François Boucher (1703–70), who as a boy had been his pupil. The best-known French artist in engraving, however, was probably Jean Honoré Fragonard (1732–1806), who specialised in Classical and allegorical themes, as Bartolozzi did. In Italy, print-making was equally fashionable, especially in Venice. Two of the greatest names in the etching of the mid 18th century were Giovanni Battista Tiepolo (1696–1770) and Giovanni Battista Piranesi (1720–78). Tiepolo concentrated on religious scenes, like the painters of the Renaissance, and Piranesi, who spent many years in Rome, profited by the revival of interest in Classical times, stimulated by the archaeological discoveries at Pompeii and Herculaneum. He produced a whole series of etchings of the ruins of ancient Rome and brought them to life by inserting people in 18th-dress, walking about the toppled pillars, sitting under the derelict triumphal arches, even tending animals in the deserted spaces of the Forum. Copies of Piranesi's prints abound both in Italy and elsewhere in Europe.

AMUSEMENTS CHAMPÊTRES
Gravé d'après le Tableau original Peint par Watteau,
de mesme grandeur

RURIS DELICIÆ
Sculptæ juxtà Exemplar Ejusdem magnitudinis
à Watteavo Depictum

Painted by Sir Joshua Reynolds.   Engraved by F. Bartolozzi R.A.

Jane Countess of Harrington
Lord Viscount Petersham & the Hon.ble Lincoln Stanhope.

Publish'd Mar. 15. 1784 by F. Bartolozzi &c.

MOUNTING GUARD,
St JAMES'S PARK.

109
Aquatint of Thomas Rowlandson's *Mounting Guard, St. James's Park*. Victoria and Albert Museum, London.

110
The Tower of London, an etching by Wenceslaus Hollar (1607-77), who introduced the process of etching into England. British Museum, London.

111
The Bathos, engraved by William Hogarth. Bibliothèque Nationale, Paris.

American prints offer a rich field for the collector. The earlier Colonists imported prints from Europe, but towards the end of the 17th century a few local engravings were made. Importation continued, however, until the War of Independence. After that a number of skilled engravers emigrated from Britain and put their hands to print-making. They were in demand not only to record some of the great highlights of the war which had been such a triumph for the Colonists, but also to produce landscapes and urban views which emigrants delighted in sending home to their families in Britain. Many of the landscapes were aquatints and the colour was very good. Among the best-known engravers were William Birch (1755–1835) and his son, Thomas (1779–1851), of Boston. They produced line-engravings of scenes in Philadelphia which are sought by collectors.

Battle scenes of the War of 1812–14 with Britain were also popular, especially naval engagements. Thomas Birch, who had turned to water-colour painting early in the 19th century, depicted a number of famous battles, and engravings were made of these by several artists, such as *The Capture of the British Frigate Gurriere*. These scenes can occasionally be bought cheaply on either side of the Atlantic. Perhaps the most exciting American prints are the railroad ones, but they are mainly too late to qualify for inclusion in this book.

Castrum Royale Londinense   vulgo   the TOWER.

TAIL PIECE.

Design'd and Engrav'd by Wm Hogarth.   THE BATHOS,   Publish'd according to Act of Parliam^t. March 3^d 1764.

or Manner of Sinking, in Sublime Paintings,

inscribed to the Dealers in Dark Pictures.

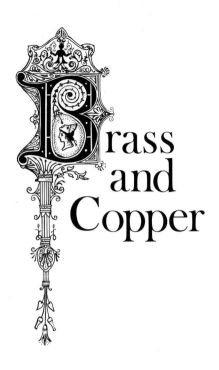

Brass and Copper

No country antique dealer would consider he was running his shop properly unless he stocked a good selection of brass and copper articles. In London alone there are at least a dozen shops given over almost exclusively to them. And yet, unless an article can be proved to be of earlier date than about 1600, it is unlikely to have very great value, at least at present. So you could start collecting brass and copper now quite easily, and perhaps your heirs will ultimately reap the benefit!

Before starting to collect copper, it would be as well to clear up one or two points about its manufacturing history. It is one of the oldest metals known to man, and it is a constituent of bronze. The Bronze Age more or less marks the period when man first became civilised. Copper, either in its natural state or as part of an alloy or mixture, has thus been in use for 6,000 years at least.

In Britain up to the end of the 17th century, articles were made of thick copper beaten out with a battery hammer, and the colour, after polishing, was generally very pale. Beating was not of a very high degree of skill, and the surface of containers, for example, had many flaws. At the end of the century beating techniques improved and there were far fewer flaws. The colour, too, became more red, but the metal remained thickish. Then, in about 1730, manufacturers began to roll copper, and the resulting products were much thinner, much more red, and nearly flawless. From about 1775 copper hollow-ware, that is, vessels for holding liquids, were sometimes stamped with ornamental designs. This was done by beating the copper from the reverse side of the sheet into specially cut dies. As the vessels were often made to hold liquids for drinking, or at least to reach the mouth, the poisonous copper surfaces inside were plated with tin. This was also the case with saucepans, preserving pans and such like. Early in the 19th century copper vessels were made of spun copper, that is, sheet thin and malleable enough for spinning on a lathe.

It is therefore possible to give rough dates to copper articles, but a word of warning. There is not much left of copperware of the more ordinary household variety that is older than about 1800. Most earlier pieces are in museums, and their dates can be proved. Coal scuttles and kettles, for example, even if they conform to the rules, that is, are thick, pale, and have flaws, are almost always skilful mid or late 19th-century copies of earlier styles. There are some experts outside a museum or important house who state that no coal scuttle or kettle exists that can be dated before 1837.

Principal articles of copper still available, even if sometimes they are only good copies, are ale measures,

112

American brass trivet, with an eagle motif, on an iron stand. It was made in about 1780. American Museum in Britain, Claverton Manor, Bath.

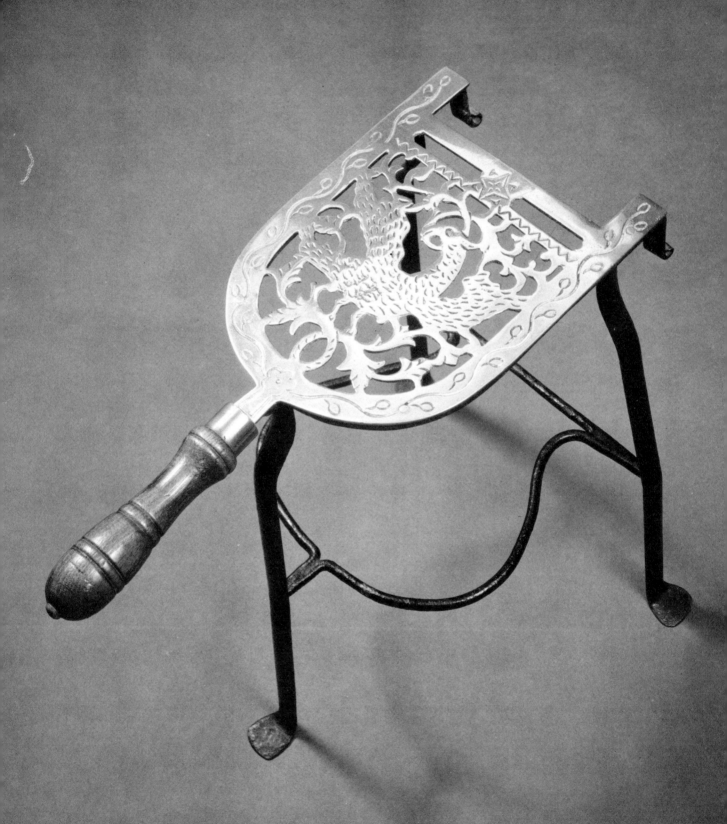

113

114

saucepans, coffee pots, warming pans, candle-holders (not candlesticks) and preserving pans. Naturally a variety of other articles were made, such as trays, finger bowls and goblets. Ale measures came in sets from half gallon down to a dram or tablespoonful. Full sets of 18th-century ale measures are extremely rare, and copied sets, which are expensive, can be seen in many country inns. You will notice that the copper is thin and so much more dented than it need be that at first sight the copy looks like the genuine article.

The warming pan is an interesting household article. **116** It dates back to the Middle Ages, when the pan part was of brass or bronze and it had a metal handle. James II's son, by his second wife Mary of Modena, was thought by some not to have been her child but a substitute brought into the royal confinement room in a warming pan. It is unlikely that it would have been a copper pan, however, for these do not appear to have come in until about 1700, when they had beech handles well turned and sometimes lacquered in black. Since the advent of the hot-water bottle and the electric blanket, these pans are no longer functional, but they do look attractive when hung on a wall, especially if they are kept sparkling clean.

The other popular metal was brass. This is an alloy of copper and zinc, the zinc being obtained for centuries from calamine mineral from Somerset or from the district around Liège in Belgium (there was a large brass trade there for a long time).

A considerable number of articles have been made in **120** brass. It is harder and so less susceptible to denting. But it loses its brilliance very quickly, and in the old days it was given regular and frequent polishing. Old pieces therefore ought to show signs of wear, which would be difficult – and uneconomical – to imitate. In about 1770 various attempts were made to protect brass from dulling, and a lacquer was developed. Nowadays cellulose can be used, but it is not recommended unless you know that it is definitely a type that is harmless and can be removed with ease.

Medieval brass articles, such as fire-dogs and ecclesiastical items such as crucifixes, plates and

113
Two horse brasses of the first half of the 19th century.

114
Two pairs of late 18th-century English brass candlesticks. The square corners of the front pair reveal considerable wear.

115
Early 18th-century American copper and wood candle-holder. The holder was jammed horizontally into a wall stud or door lintel. American Museum in Britain, Claverton Manor, Bath.

116
Typical late 18th-century English warming pan of copper with turned wood handle.

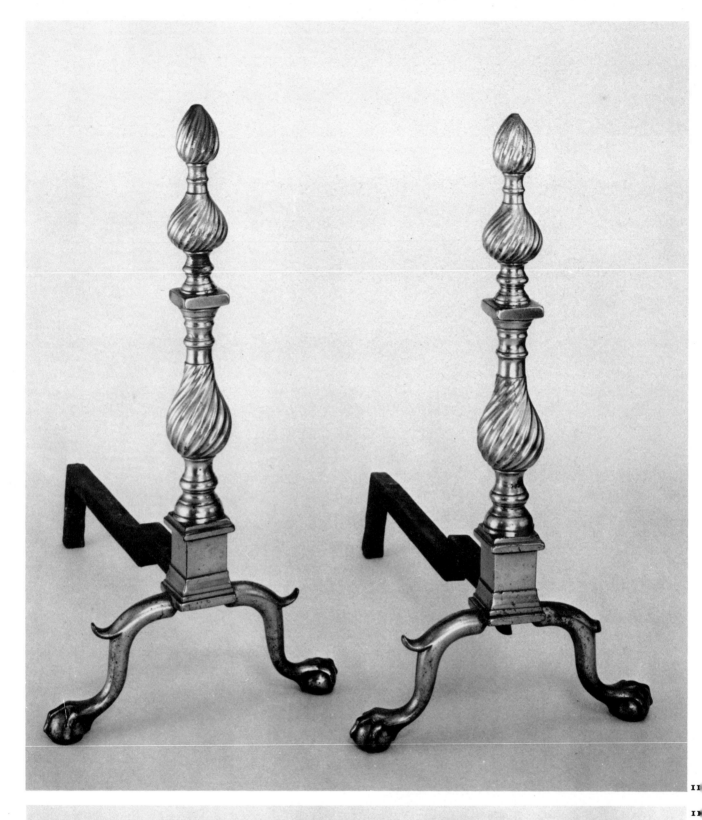

chalices, are found extremely rarely outside museums or old buildings, and if they were obtainable, would be very expensive. But after about 1600 brass began to be made in great quantity, and, like copper, can be collected quite cheaply. What is more, the variety is greater.

Perhaps the most famous article made in brass in the past was the candlestick, and this is not surprising since every house had to have lighting of some kind. Most 17th-century candlesticks of brass had wide, round, inverted trumpet bases. Half-way up the stem was a special candle-wax catcher, for the earlier candle-holder lips were hardly thicker than the holders. Then, at the end of the century, someone thought of bending the lip over at right angles outwards, so that it acted as a candle-wax catcher. A little later, the lip was part of a removable tube which slotted inside the top of the stick. The central catcher then disappeared. A stick with a catcher in the middle or thereabouts would therefore be a good find.

At the same time, that is, early in the 18th century, stick bases began to vary. Sometimes they would be square-shaped with the corners cut off, or octagonal, or shaped as a pattern of leaves. The stems, too, sported a variety of shapes, some not unlike the baluster stems of early 18th-century drinking glasses. In the Classical Revival period following Robert Adam, in the second half of the century, stems became square, with fluting or reeding, occasionally rising to architectural capitals, such as the Corinthian acanthus-leaf type. Vase-shaped stems also appeared.

It is not of course easy to spot the difference between genuine and fake articles, but a rough guide is that up to about 1670 the stem and candle-holder were cast as one piece and attached to the base by screw thread or tenon through the hole in the centre. After this time the two pieces tended to be brazed together at the join between base and stem. This persisted almost throughout the 18th century, and in the 19th century makers returned to making casts in one piece or to assembling candle-sticks from several pieces. Mouldings should have been considerably softened by years of wear and would be hard to imitate.

Another popular article for collecting is the horse brass, though it is by no means easy even for the expert to distinguish between the 18th- and early 19th-century genuine ones and the mass-produced variety

that has been turned out since about 1880. Old horse brasses were usually fitted to the harness of the horse and should show signs of wear underneath, where they rubbed against the leather. Many also had two short pins brazed on the underside with which the craftsman held the whole brass in a vice before cutting and polishing the design. The brass had flaws, little crevices which collected dirt. But it is not very difficult to fake horse brasses, and the last resort is to depend upon the honesty of the dealer or the knowledge of an expert.

Fire-dogs, otherwise called andirons, have been in use since the Middle Ages, when they were made of wrought iron. Brass came into use for decorating and surmounting them from about 1500, but the stand and the feet remained in iron. Fire-dogs made entirely of brass, therefore, are not genuine, and were probably made in Edwardian times. In the 18th century, when coal began to replace wood for heating, fenders were invented to prevent hot coal embers scattering across and scorching the wooden floor or the carpeting in front of the fire. They were made in iron, and also in brass and iron. Generally, the front piece was of pierced brass, supported by iron brackets and standing on an iron base plate. Many of the designs were Classical, after the Adam revival. At this time, too, some fenders incorporated stands for the fire-irons, and so the need for separate dogs declined.

Brass fenders abound, and good ones, probably early **118** 19th-century imitations, can be found. It is of course difficult to determine their age, as the skill of the 19th-century makers was very great.

Another item of brass which you can collect is the trivet. These were stands for kettles or saucepans by firesides. They had fittings for the bars of grates, or legs on which the trivet could stand independently. The 17th- and early 18th-century forms were usually round, with brass tops. Then they became more square with a rounded end, out of which protruded a handle. This trivet was mounted on four legs. The surface was often pierced or otherwise decorated in most intricate patterns, and sometimes the plain pieces of the brass were engraved.

Very little brass or copper was made in America **115** before the War of Independence. What was needed by the early immigrants was generally imported from Europe. But, as with glass and china, after the war there was a spontaneous rush to design and manufacture household and decorative utensils in brass and copper. In 1780 James Emerson fused zinc and copper in the **112** ratio one to two and produced a very high-quality brass which had a golden hue. It was soft to beat out and could be produced in thin sheets for easy use. An Emerson piece is hard to find, anywhere, but later articles, made in brass according to his formula, can be picked up and are worth collecting. In 1790 the Waterbury Brass Works were opened in Connecticut, and a

117
Pair of American brass andirons (fire-dogs) made by Paul Revere and Son in Boston, late in the 18th century. Metropolitan Museum of Art, New York; Sylmaris Collection. Gift of George Coe Granes, 1930.

118
Early 18th-century pierced and engraved brass fender. Victoria and Albert Museum, London.

119
Copper kettle of about 1820. Royal Pavilion, Brighton.

120
Collection of brass handles for furniture. The first six (across) date roughly from 1660 to 1714, the second six (across) from 1714 to 1760 and the remainder from 1760 to 1830. A considerable number of imitations have been made in the last 120 years. Victoria and Albert Museum, London.

few years later Paul Revere, the silver expert, was designing and making a variety of brass articles including fire-dogs.

Copper collectors in America still search for late 18th- and early 19th-century weathervanes. These were often made of two or more sheets of copper brazed together at the edges, and cut out to form the figures required, such as cockerels, fishes, ships, horses, and even grasshoppers. Coppersmiths also produced with great skill those items so widely used in Britain: coal scuttles, kettles (in America they often had swinging handles) and preserving pans.

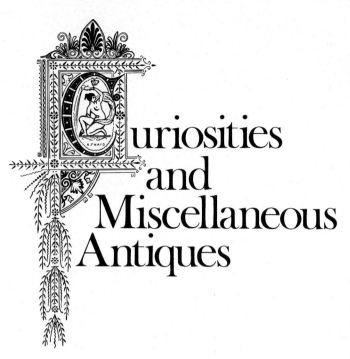

Curiosities and Miscellaneous Antiques

Apart from the main fields of antiques, there is an almost limitless range of old things which can be collected and which are variously described as bric-à-brac, curios, curiosities, objets d'art, junk, even 'junque'. None of these phrases is very suitable, not least because none of them embraces the whole range. 'Miscellaneous antiques' is too long, but 'antiquaria' might be appropriate. A full list of such antiques would be impracticable in a book of this size, and there are already several books available which are more or less devoted to the subject.

Collecting such miscellanea can be enormous fun. It can also be an investment for the future. One often hears on radio feature programmes, or reads in magazines, of someone who has amassed over 500 chamber pots, or, like Lord Boyd, walking sticks, or family games, or musical boxes. Sometimes a collection of one kind, comprising otherwise unsensational items, can realise a great deal of money because it is a 'collection' and somewhere in the world somebody else is making a collection of similar items. This is the kind of chance you take with almost any type of collection. If the articles are decorative, and perhaps functional as well, then it will be no great loss to you if ten years later you find that your collection is not valuable enough to pay for a new car. In the long term, however, the collection must prove to be more valuable than the total cost of it was to you originally.

Here is a short list of the kind of articles which are still eminently collectable. Then follows a longer description of some nine articles which you may consider worthwhile collecting when you have looked around in shops and auction rooms and read a few more books. They are: apothecaries' jars, barometers, bellarmines (stoneware bottles with long necks, the front of which is decorated with the mask of a man with a beard), bird-cages, buttons, bygones (articles no longer in use, such as old-fashioned agricultural tools; there is a fine collection of these at the Troubadour Restaurant in London), cameos, chessmen, card cases (in ivory, silver, fine wood, papier mâché, or mother-of-pearl), children's furniture, commemorative pottery, dolls, family games, fitted boxes, locks and keys, maps,

121

A selection of antique buttons: (a) English button of about 1800, of cut and polished steel set into mother-of-pearl; (b) early 19th-century German painted porcelain button edged with gold paint; (c) European fixé-painted glass button with glass dome; (d) 18th-century English paste button in a silver setting; (e) early 19th-century English livery button in mercury gilt on a bell-metal base; (f) early 19th-century North European peasant's silver button with toggle; (g) 19th-century mercury gilt button with the legend 'God Save the King', struck to commemorate the recovery of George III from one of his bouts of ill-health; (h) early 19th-century regimental button with the insignia of the Royal Flintshire Militia, in mercury gilt on a bell-metal base.

122
Miniature bureau-bookcase probably made by an apprentice cabinet-maker in the early part of the 18th century. These apprentice pieces are not very common.

123
American Betty lamp of the 18th century. American Museum in Britain, Claverton Manor, Bath.

124
(Left) English pewter half-pint 'bellied' measure of about 1770. (Right) pewter pint measure of the end of the 18th century, stamped with later excise marks of William IV and Victoria.

3

4

miniature furniture, musical boxes, old scientific instruments, pewter tankards and plates, prisoner-of-war work (things made by French prisoners held in Britain between 1756 and 1815), playing cards, ships in bottles, samplers, swords and halberds, tea caddies, vinaigrettes, walking sticks, witch balls, and wickerwork. **124 130**

There are of course many, many more things. As this book is limited to antiques, that is, things made before 1830–40, we must leave out a host of Victoriana which, if collected now, will certainly appreciate in value.

Barometers The barometer was invented in about 1642 by Evangelista Torricelli, an Italian scientist who had been secretary to the great Galileo. A copy of his first instrument is preserved in the Science Museum, London. It is stick-shaped, and is the forerunner of stick barometers. Robert Hooke, the English scientist, invented a wheel barometer, and the derivatives of that are 'banjo' barometers.

Wheel barometers, with dial face and hands, were perhaps the most common type made, for about 200 years, and in their earliest times they were designed by some of the most famous clock-makers of the day, such as Thomas Tompion and Joseph Knibb. Such specimens are rare and would fetch huge prices on the market. But in the 18th century more and more wheel barometers were made, many by little-known craftsmen. These barometers have a thermometer needle as well, generally in the top half of the case.

The casing of barometers received as much attention as the works, and a great variety of decoration is found: bow-fronted with architectural pediment for the stick-type, and lyre-shaped with marquetry or inlay (often with the shell motif) for the wheel-type. You can find wheel barometers of the 18th century, described probably as 'Sheraton', but in fact having nothing whatever to do with him, for a moderate price, but when buying one you should be careful to see that it works properly. Barometers are not cheap to repair. The temperature-reading on the mercury thermometer should normally be accurate, unless the glass has been damaged, in which case it will be affected only slightly by room temperature. **131**

127

125
Selection of English card cases of the early 19th century. (Left to right) tortoiseshell with ivory decoration; silver filigree; mother-of-pearl; mother-of-pearl.

126
Swiss musical box of about 1830, decorated with strings of silver and discs of mother-of-pearl. This box plays four waltzes. Private Collection.

127
Late 18th-century American pierced tin lantern. These are much sought after in the United States. American Museum in Britain, Claverton Manor, Bath.

129

128
Doll of the Queen Anne period, with wooden head and peg legs.
The cradle dates from the late 18th century. Private Collection.

129
Pair of early 19th-century American candle-shades of painted
parchment standing on adjustable wooden stands. American
Museum in Britain, Claverton Manor, Bath.

130
Model of a man o'war made in about 1810, a fine example of 'prisoner-of-war work'. Prisoners captured in the various wars with France between 1756 and 1815, and confined in British prisons, sometimes produced articles such as boxes and models. These are usually referred to as 'prisoner-of-war work'. National Maritime Museum, Greenwich, London.

131
English mahogany barometer of the late 18th century, with tulipwood inlay. Private Collection.

Buttons At first you might not consider buttons worth collecting, but in fact a group of buttons with painted scenes under glass fetched £6,613 (about $15,871) at Sotheby's in 1961. Today there is a shop in central London, called *The Button Queen*, which is almost exclusively devoted to their sale. In the United States there is a National Button Society, which publishes a regular button bulletin.

Buttons were made to fasten or decorate clothes, and since the majority were intended for prominent positions on the costume, no amount of skill was spared in their making. Nor does there seem to be much limit to the types of material used. To mention but a few, buttons have been made in gold, silver, brass, bronze, steel, enamel, porcelain (plain or painted), mother-of-pearl, glass, bone, wood, ivory, papier mâché, tortoiseshell, paste, cut-steel insert in mother-of-pearl, transfer-printed china, leather, sea-shell, and precious and semi-precious stones. Buttons were also made to represent rank or position: to mark regimental insignia (military buttons alone are extensive enough to warrant collecting on their own merits) or livery insignia, to commemorate events, to represent sporting club membership, even to act as personal identification. Buttons are generally so small, however, that unless one is well experienced in button collecting, it is very difficult to judge their age at all accurately. In identifying military buttons some clue may be afforded if the insignia is of a regiment which has been disbanded and if the dates of existence of the regiment are known.

American collectors are particularly interested in those buttons which in some way or other record the story of the Republic since the War of Independence, such as those celebrating Lafayette's trip to the United States, or the first railways, or regiments which fought against the British in the War of 1812–14. Prices for American collectors vary from as little as a dollar to more than a hundred dollars. In Britain the scale is perhaps a little less extensive, and the cheapest 18th-century button will cost about thirty shillings.

Chessmen Chess has been played in Europe and the East since the Middle Ages, and it probably originated in China. The earliest chessmen were made of the most luxurious materials, such as ivory faced with gold and inlaid with jewels, or fine enamel, or rare woods, or ebony. In the first centuries of chess the 'men' often represented real or imaginary people. The kings, for example, were fine characterisations of living monarchs, complete with crowns and robes, the knights were mounted on horseback, and the pawns might be soldiers or citizens, possibly a selection of important local people including doctors, priests, lawyers, and so on. William Caxton, who introduced printing into England in the reign of Edward IV, describes the game and its pieces in one of his earliest books.

Right down to the 19th century, sets of men were also made representing two opposing sides in some famous war, such as Crusaders and Saracens, or Indians and East India Company officials, or Roundheads and Cavaliers. The colours were as a rule basically red and white or black and white, and these colours have persisted, although red and white are not so common now.

Some 17th-century pieces were made of iron or brass or pewter, or even lead, and from time to time a set might have pewter on one side and bronze on the other. In the 18th century some very fine porcelain sets were made by Meissen and other porcelain factories. The pottery sets by Wedgwood, in blue and white jasper, are delightful, but they are very expensive.

Since a great many sets were made at one time or another, you could quite easily begin to collect them. It will not be a cheap hobby; even a fairly ordinary set of red and white ivory pieces fetched £10 (about $24) at a sale in Torquay in October 1969. You will find dealers who specialise in chessmen; one of the best known in London is in Lansdowne Place.

Fitted boxes In the 18th century, and to a greater extent in the 19th, people liked to have tools and other items of equipment for a variety of activities neatly stored in boxes, not unlike the 'do-it-yourself' kits of the present century. For example, many houses had their own medicine dispensary in a special fitted box, which was called an apothecary's box. This was usually a wooden box, very well made, and beautifully fitted internally, with compartments for bottles or phials, and a drawer or space for apparatus for making up one's own medicine according to a doctor's prescription.

131

This apparatus included a small pestle and mortar, a pair of hand scales with weights, a spatula and a pair of forceps. These boxes came in many sizes and shapes: rectangular or square, tall or squat.

Another kind of apothecary's box was the type used **134** by doctors and surgeons on their rounds or in infirmaries, hospitals and sick-bays. This was more elaborate, with spaces for instruments. Another type is the ship's box, but these would not be at all easy to find, for they tended to disappear when ships were broken up and the contents sold for scrap.

A number of other boxes were made and fitted out for various uses, such as writing boxes, toilet boxes and sewing boxes, but these are more common in the 19th century and not very many qualify as antiques. When they do, they are often rarities and therefore expensive. A great deal of skill was put into the design and the decoration of these boxes, and you will find them in mahogany inlaid with satinwood or boxwood, some with marquetry of a high standard, or with ebony, brass or ivory inlay.

Maps In the chapter on prints one of the categories not mentioned comprises old maps. These are very attractive indeed to have about the house, and if they are really old they are also valuable. Maps were engraved or etched like prints, and the colouring was generally done by hand after printing. The earliest surviving maps in Britain date from the 16th century— that is, the kind you will normally find in shops or at sales (older ones are now exclusive to museums or private collections). The names most widely associated with 16th- and 17th-century maps are Saxton, Norden and Speed. These and other cartographers produced a splendid variety of maps of the counties of England and Wales, and later Scotland and Ireland, and it is interesting to look at a 17th-century map of, for example, Suffolk, and to see how accurate a view the

132 (*page 126*)
Part of a rare set of French carved ivory chessmen of about 1750, together with chessboard of leather.

133 (*page 127*)
Fitted military dressing box with mahogany case, of about 1820.

134
Apothecary's box or medicine chest, a typical fitted box, with its contents. This one was made in about 1750. Wellcome Historical Medical Museum, London.

135
English silver chessmen made by E. Fennel in 1815.

cartographers had of the geography of the county in those far-off days. It is also fun to see familiar towns, great houses, rivers and roads, their names perhaps spelt differently from now. Road maps were also produced in these late Tudor and early Stuart times, usually in scroll form, that is, a row of scroll-ended panels each depicting a section of the road being illustrated. These can still be bought quite cheaply, but they may not be original or even early editions. Good examples of early maps are not common, but a vast number of reproductions have been made over the centuries. They have also been faked.

In the 18th century new and more accurate maps were made which revealed the gradual industrialisation of Britain, showing, for example, the network of canals or, in the 19th century, the new grid of railways.

If you want to extend your horizons to other regions, maps of Europe, Asia, Africa and the world, as our ancestors saw them, go back at least 400 years. The earliest maps of the world are decorated with a great deal of superstitious imagery, such as pictures of gryphons, dolphins, sea-monsters, and Hell, and with well-placed injunctions to avoid wild beasts or cannibals or whirlpools. In the 15th century Europeans believed that down the West African coast, in the neighbourhood of the Gold Coast (now Ghana), the sea boiled and flames engulfed all ships which wandered there, and these fears were not stilled until the Portuguese

136

136
County map of Suffolk by John Speed, 1610.

137
American sampler of 1774. American Museum in Britain,
Claverton Manor, Bath.

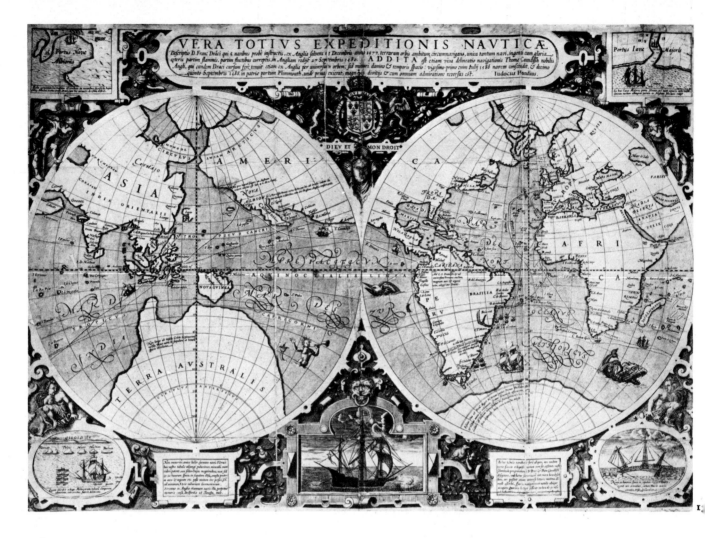

VERA TOTIVS EXPEDITIONIS NAVTICÆ.

138
Late 16th-century map engraved by Jodocus Hondius and showing the sea voyages of Sir Francis Drake and Thomas Cavendish.

139
Late 18th-century flintlock blunderbuss by Rigby and Son. This has a brass barrel fitted with under-action spring bayonet, which is released by pulling the spring catch placed in front of the trigger guard.

140
American Colt revolver of 1849. Winchester Gun Museum, Connecticut.

captain, Gil Eannes, and his successors dared to round the west coast towards Nigeria and then cross the Equator. It is difficult to be helpful about prices for these kinds of maps, and the best course, in Britain, is to consult the Map Collectors' Circle, in London.

Old Pewter You will see pewter plates and tankards everywhere, especially in old inns, for pewter has been used for utensils for many centuries. It is an alloy of tin with lead, antimony, bismuth or copper. There is a lot of pewter about, some of it old and some of it good 19th-century reproduction. While it was not normally marked, certainly not in the same way as silver was, some markings were used which can help to date

occasional pieces. For this you should consult one of the books on pewter mentioned in the bibliography.

Pewter appears to have been made in three basic forms: plate, trifle and lay. Plate pewter was used mainly for the flatter pieces, such as plates and trivets, and it was made up of about four parts of tin to one of copper, with a small amount of lead. Trifle pewter was of a slightly softer consistency, made up of about five parts of tin to one of antimony, and was used to make tankards, porringers, cups and other vessels. Since many of the vessels were associated with drinking, lead was excluded altogether. Lay pewter, regarded as the cheapest kind, contained a great deal of lead.

Pewter offers a wide scope for collection, and in view of the number of experts in the field, you should not find it difficult to acquire a knowledge of it. After 1824, drinking cups and tankards of pewter (and of other materials as well) had to be stamped with the capacity of the vessel, together with the initials of the reigning monarch. It has been said that since that regulation the quality and value of pewter in general began to decline.

Samplers Quite a number of articles made by our ancestors for, or in, the home, are now used for different purposes from those for which they were first designed. One of them is the sampler. It was originally embroidered, well over 300 years ago, as a kind of

reference panel for types of stitch, specimens of pattern, and range of colours. The linen was stretched over a frame which was square or rectangular in shape. Coloured silks were used, and, much later, coloured wools. The most usual patterns were simple, geometrical ones, vaguely resembling the inlay found in English furniture of the early 17th century, and also some motifs from nature, such as birds and flowers. By the 18th century the making of samplers had become widely accepted as a children's exercise. Children were set to embroider a motto or perhaps the letters of the alphabet in capital and small letters. Occasionally the length of the alphabet was misjudged and the last few letters are squeezed together at the right-hand end or wander up the side. These samplers were as a rule signed and dated.

It does not follow that all 18th-century samplers are children's exercise work, for they were also embroidered by fine needlewomen and enclosed in frames, like pictures deliberately intended for decorative purposes. The cost of samplers varies very much according to design, skill of embroidery, material and date. In America, **137** samplers began to be made early in the 18th century, later than in Britain, but they follow the same patterns in general. The idea clearly derived from immigrant families in New England. Examples made after about 1800 are easy to buy, but the earlier ones are becoming rare.

Swords and pole arms Arms and armour are a wide enough field to justify the books that have been written about them (see the bibliography). But in this review only two collecting items, swords and pole arms, are mentioned.

Swords go back to the earliest days of civilisation, but the only kinds you are likely to find on the market, which are not too expensive, are some of those dating from about 1400. The usual sword of the late Middle Ages, such as that used perhaps in the Wars of the Roses in England, is straight, sharpened on both edges, and with a cross guard or guillon. It was generally made in three or four lengths, the average being about 4 feet (1·2 m.), but the longest extending to 6 feet (1·8 m.). The long type required two hands to wield it with any effect, but it was a most lethal weapon, for it could cut through mail and armour plate. If you tap the top of a helmet of the period with a knuckle, you may get some idea of the almost indescribable noise that accompanied a clash between, say, the heavy infantry and cavalry of the Yorkists and Lancastrians at the battle of Bosworth Field in 1485.

In the 1500s new types emerged, including the light-weight rapier which evolved very largely to render the **141** 'sport' of duelling somewhat easier. The rapier had a shell-type guard, not unlike those on fencing rapiers of today, and the blade was triangular or square in section, with concave faces. The hilts and pommels of

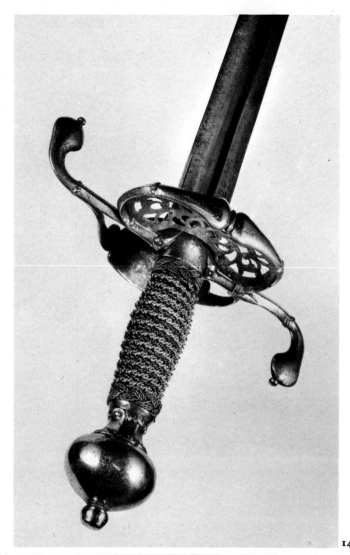

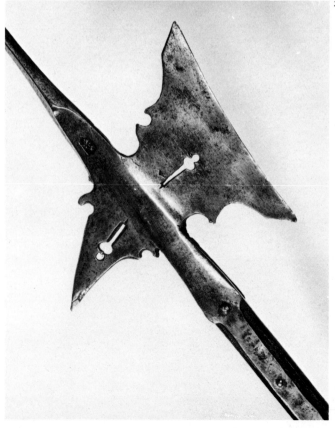

these swords were often the subject of the finest decoration, which to some extent indicates the decline in practical use of the sword in battle in the 16th century, and its increasing use in ceremonial.

Another innovation was the sabre, a sword usually provided with a curved blade and only one sharpened edge. Straight ones were also made. Sabres were fashionable as ceremonial swords in the 18th century, and you could build up a collection of these, for the scabbards, as well as the swords themselves, are often finely decorated. They occasionally appear in sales quite cheaply, and I have seen them in the Portobello Road, London, for moderate prices.

Pole arms are basically cut-and-thrust weapons mounted on very long handles. The best known in the public mind is the pike, followed closely by the halberd. Others, less well known, are the war-hammer, which has a sharp-pointed fluke, the lance, and the partizan, which has a long, triangular-shaped head with two pointed lugs at the base. The pike is a sort of spear with an assegai-type head; in the 17th century the handle became as long as 20 feet (6·02 m.). It was particularly useful to unseat riders wearing full armour, who at best sat most uneasily on horseback. The halberd has an axe-like blade with a spike (called a fluke) projecting out at right-angles to the handle and opposite the axe-blade. There is another spike arrangement at the top. This makes the halberd a cut-and-thrust weapon, and for 200 years or more it was a most important weapon in any battle. A pair of crossed halberds would look splendid on the wall of the drawing room or in the hall, but the dimensions of the house would have to be larger than average, for, like the pike, the halberd is long-handled.

Pole arms occasionally appear in sales, and there are one or two dealers who specialise in them. Perhaps the most comprehensive range of these weapons, and indeed of all antique weapons and armour, in London is obtainable at P. C. L. German in Edgware Road.

Tea caddies Tea first came to Britain in the 17th century. By the 18th, most upper-class people were drinking it regularly, although they had to pay ten shillings or more for one pound of it, which is more than for most brands today. It was, therefore, something of of a luxury, and it had to be kept from the servants. As a result, containers evolved which had locks and keys. These came to be called tea caddies, after the *kati*, which was the Malayan measure of weight of approximately 1·2 lbs., (543·6 gms.).

Tea caddies were of a variety of shapes—square, rectangular, hexagonal, vase-like, or oval—and they had vaulted, domed or rectilinear tops. Inside, the caddy might be divided into two or three compartments, for two kinds of tea and, possibly, a bowl in which to blend them. The bowl, usually of glass, might be used for sugar instead.

141
German sword or rapier of the 16th century, with pierced guard and wooden grip bound with silver wire.

142
Fine 16th-century German halberd blade, showing the armourer's mark. It is dated about 1540.

143
English-made 19th-century tulipwood and kingwood tea poy, with gilt-bronze mounts and gallery, in the style of a French Louis XV work table. Author's Collection.

144
Late 18th-century satinwood tea caddy inlaid with other woods.
Victoria and Albert Museum, London.

Wooden tea caddies, plain or inlaid with boxwood or satinwood or with marquetry of various patterns, or veneered in tortoiseshell, have survived in some quantity. Examples dating from the third quarter of the 18th century can be bought quite cheaply. Occasionally, a caddy of larger size was mounted on a pillar with three legs, or on a base with four legs, to make a piece of furniture that could have a number of uses today. This was sometimes called a 'tea poy', but it is really an early 19th-century idea. Some were of rosewood and were very attractive. In England early in the 19th century it was fashionable to make copies of 18th-century French furniture, and the occasional tea poy was made in the shape of a workbox of the Louis XV or transitional periods. Such pieces are not common, however, and would be very expensive to buy today.

Bibliography

General
Bedford, J., *Looking in Junk Shops*. London, 1961.
Bedford, J., *More Looking in Junk Shops*. London, Ed. 1968.
Boger, L. A. and H. B., *Dictionary of Antiques and the Decorative Arts*. London, 1969.
Butler, J. T., *American Antiques*. New York, 1965.
Cole, A. K., *The Golden Guide to American Antiques*. New York, 1967.
Hughes, G. Bernard, *The Antique Collector's Pocket Book*. New York, 1968.
Ramsay, L. G. G., Ed., *The Complete Encyclopedia of Antiques*. London, 1967.
Savage, G., *Forgeries, Fakes and Reproductions*. London, 1963.
Speck, G. E. and Sutherland, E., *English Antiques*. London, 1969.
The Connoisseur's Complete Period Guides. London, 1968.

Furniture
Edwards, Ralph, *Georgian Furniture*. London, 1958.
Fastnedge, Ralph, *English Furniture Styles, from 1500 to 1830*. London, 1955.
Hayward, Helena, Ed., *World Furniture*. London, 1965.
Nagel, C., *American Furniture, 1680–1850*. London, 1950
Nickerson, D., *English Furniture of the 18th Century*. London, 1963.
Packer, Charles, *Paris Furniture*. Newport, Monmouthshire, 1956.
Schmitz, Hermann, *Encyclopedia of Furniture*. London, 1926.
Souchal, Genevieve, *French Eighteenth Century Furniture*. London, 1961.
Victoria and Albert Museum, *English Cabinets*. London, 1964.
Victoria and Albert Museum, *Chests of Drawers and Commodes*. London, 1960.
Victoria and Albert Museum, *Tables*. London, 1961.
Wanscher, Ole, *The Art of Furniture*. London, 1968.
Watson, F. J. B., *Louis XVI Furniture*. London, 1960.
Williams, H., *Country Furniture of Early America*. New York, 1964.

Porcelain and Pottery
Charleston, R., Ed., *World Ceramics*. London, 1968.
Earle, E. M., *China Collecting in America*. New York, 1924.
Honey, W. B., *Ceramic Art of China*. London, 1945.
Honey, W. B., *Wedgwood Ware*. London, 1948.

Mankowitz, W. and Haggar, R., *Concise Encyclopedia of English Pottery and Porcelain*. London and New York, 1957.
Marshall, H. R., *Coloured Worcester Porcelain*. Newport, Monmouthshire, 1954.
Savage, G., *Old English Porcelain*. London, 1952.
Savage, G., *18th Century German Porcelain*. London 1959.
Spargo, John, *Early American Pottery and China*. New York, 1926.
Towner, D. C., *Leeds Pottery*. London, 1963.

Glass
Bedford, J., *Bristol and Other Glass*. London, 1964.
Bedford, J., *English Crystal Glass*. London, 1966.
Davis, Frank, *The Country Life Book of Glass*. London, 1966.
Elville, E. M., *English Table Glass*. London, 1951.
Elville, E. M., *Paperweights and Other Glass Curiosities*. London, 1954.
Elville, E. M., *The Collector's Dictionary of Glass*. London, 1967.
Hughes. G. B., *Table Glass in England, Scotland and Ireland from the 16th Century to 1820*. London, 1956.
Kampfer, F. and Beyer, K. G., *Glass: A World History*. London, 1967.
Lee, R., *Early American Pressed Glass*. New York, 1946.
Watkins, L. W., *American Glass and Glassmaking*. New York, 1950.
Westropp, M. S. D., *Irish Glass*. London, 1920.
Wills, Geoffrey, *The Country Life Pocket Book of Glass*. London, 1966.

Silver and Silver Plate
Banister, J., *An Introduction to Old English Silver*. London, 1965.
Bradbury, F., *Old Sheffield Plate Makers' Marks, 1740–1860*. London, 1932.
Curran, M., *Collecting English Silver*. London, 1963.
Hughes, G. B., *Small Antique Silverware*. London, 1957.
Phillips, J. M., *American Silver*. London and New York, 1949.
Ramsay, L. G. G., *Antique English Silver and Plate*. London, 1962.
Rupert, C. G., *Apostle Spoons*. London, 1929.
Shure, D. S., *Hester Bateman, Queen of English Silversmiths*. New York, 1959.
Wyler, S. B., *The Book of Old Silver*. New York, 1949.

Clocks and Watches

Baillie, G. H., *Watchmakers and Clockmakers of the World*. London, 1947.

Bruton, E., *Clocks and Watches: 1400–1900*. London, 1967.

Camerer Cuss, T., *The Country Life Book of Watches*. London, 1967.

Dreppard, C. W., *American Clocks and Clockmakers*. New York, 1956.

Joy, E. T., *The Country Life Book of Clocks*. London, 1967.

Morpugo, E., *Precious Watches*. London, 1966.

Palmer, B., *The Book of American Clocks*. New York, 1950.

Symonds, R. W., *A History of English Clocks*. London, 1947.

Symonds, R. W., *Thomas Tompion, His Life and Work*. London, 1951.

Old Prints

Brigham, C. S., *Paul Revere's Engravings*. American Antiquarian Society, Worcester, Massachusetts. 1954.

Dreppard, C., *Early American Prints*. New York, 1950.

Gray, B., *The English Print*. London, 1937.

Hayter, S. W., *About Prints*. London, 1962.

Hind, A., *A History of Engraving and Etching*. London and New York, 1963.

Lumsden, E. S., *The Art of Etching*. Philadelphia, 1926.

Weber, W., *The History of Lithography*. New York, 1965.

Wolf, E. C., *Rowlandson and His Illustrations of 18th Century English Literature*. Copenhagen, 1945.

Copper and Brass

Burgess, F. W., *Chats on Old Copper and Brass*. London, 1954.

Fuller, J., *The Art of Coppersmithing*. New York, 1911.

Hartfield, G., *Horse Brasses*. London, 1965.

Hughes, G. B., *Horse Brasses*. London, 1962.

Kaufmann, H. J., *Early American Copper, Tin and Brass*. New York, 1950.

Lindsay, J. S., *Iron and Brass Implements of the English and American Home*. Stamford, Conn., 1964.

Wills, G., *Collecting Copper and Brass*. London, 1962.

Wills, G., *The Book of Copper and Brass*. London, 1968.

Curiosities and Miscellaneous Antiques

Albert, L. S., *The Complete Button Book*. New York, 1949.

Beel, G. H. and E. F., *Old English Barometers*. Winchester, 1952.

Bedford, J., *Pewter*. London, 1965.

Blair, C., *European and American Arms*. London, 1964.

Cottrell, H. H., *Old Pewter, Its Makers and Marks in England, Scotland and Ireland*. London, 1965.

Ellacott, S. E., *Armour and Blade*. London, 1962.

Hammond, Alex, *The Book of Chessmen*. London, 1950.

Hayward, J. F., *Swords and Daggers*. London, 1951.

Lee, R. J., *English County Maps*. London, 1955.

Mackett-Beeson, A. E. J., *Chessmen*. London, 1968.

Middleton, W. E. K., *The History of the Barometer*. Baltimore 1964.

Radford, P. J., *Antique Maps*. Portsmouth, Hants., 1965.

Acknowledgments

Museums, Collections and Dealers
By Gracious Permission of Her Majesty the Queen 78
Arts Council of Great Britain, London 41
American Museum in Britain, Claverton Manor, Bath 35, 37, 38, 57, 68, 70, 72, 85, 86, 89, 112, 115, 123, 127, 129, 136, 137
BBC Publications, London 34, 122
Bibliothèque Nationale, Paris 111
British Museum, London 54, 107, 110
Brooklyn Museum, New York 84
Dr Robert Burnett, England 126
The Button Queen, London 121
Camerer Cuss and Co., London 96, 99, 100
Château de Champs, France 11
Christie Manson and Woods Ltd., London 5, 6, 7, 73, 77, 81
City of Liverpool Museums, England 55
P. & D. Colnaghi Co. Ltd., London 101
Corning Museum of Glass, New York 68, 72
Delomosne and Son Ltd., London 53, 61, 62, 65, 67
Fitzwilliam Museum, Cambridge 43
Fores Ltd., London 105
Garrard and Co. Ltd., London 83, 87
P. C. L. German, London 114, 116, 124, 139, 141, 142
Gloria Antica, London 25, 125, 133
Gaby Goldscheider, London 128
H. F. du Pont Winterthur Museum, Delaware 13, 33
Hotspur Ltd., London 10, 20
John Judkyn Memorial, Freshford, England 106
A. E. J. Mackett-Beeson, London 132, 135
Mallett and Sons Ltd., London 14, 71
Mary Evans Picture Library 108
Metropolitan Museum of Art, New York 58, 74, 83, 84, 117
Musée des Arts Décoratifs, Paris 16
Musée Nationale Céramique, Sèvres, France 46
Museum of Fine Arts, Boston 36, 97
Museum of Rural Life, Reading, England 113a & b
National Trust, London 40, 44
National Maritime Museum, Greenwich 130
Newark Museum, U.S.A. 56
Parker Gallery, London 136

Partridge and Co. Ltd., London 27, 29
Percival David Foundation, London 39
Pflueger Collection, New York 42
Private Collection, London 131
Mrs. J. Renn, England 64a & b
Royal Pavilion Brighton, England 18, 19, 28, 119
Royal Scottish Museum, Edinburgh 80
Plantagenet Somerset Fry 17, 26, 50, 143
Sotheby and Co. Ltd., London 1, 9, 60
Donald Towner Collection, London 48, 52
Versailles, France 4
Victoria and Albert Museum, London 12, 22, 23, 24, 45, 47, 51, 63, 66, 69, 75, 76, 82, 91, 93, 103, 109, 118, 144
Wallace Collection, London 8, 21, 32, 90, 95
Wedgwood Museum, Josiah Wedgwood and Sons Ltd., England 49
Wellcome Medical Museum, London 134
Winchester Gun Museum, Connecticut 140
S. W. Wolsey Ltd., London 30, 31
Worshipful Company of Goldsmiths, London 79

Photographers
T. Binet, Hamlyn Group © 131
Central Press, London 2
Country Life, London 26, 94
R. B. Fleming, London 41
J. Freeman, Hamlyn Group © 22, 23, 107
Michael Holford, Hamlyn Group © 8, 17, 25, 26, 27, 29, 35, 37, 38, 44, 50, 51, 57, 68, 70, 72, 85, 86, 89, 96, 101, 105, 106, 112, 115, 116, 121, 123, 124, 125, 127, 128, 129, 132, 133, 136, 137, 139, 141, 142, 143
Jacqueline Hyde, Paris 11
Eric B. Inglefield, London 3
Edward Leigh, Cambridge 88, 92, 98
Mansell Collection, London 100
Peter Parkinson, London 79
Radio Times Hulton Picture Library 104, 138
Réalités, Connaissance des Arts, Paris 4

Index